HOLY FUCKING SHIT MORE MYTHS

By

The Rt. Hon. Dr. Nemesis R. M. Lightslayer the Magnificent, Breaker of Spines and Tweaker of Unmentionables

ISBN: 978-1-326-38340-4

Copyright © 2015 Dr. Nemesis R. M. Lightslayer
All rights reserved.

THIS BOOK IS DEDICATED TO KIERON MOTHERFUCKING GILLEN, FOR HAVING AN ATTITUDE TO MYTHOLOGY THAT SHOULD BE MORE FUCKING COMMON.

THIS IS PROBABLY A TERRIBLE MYTHTAKE.

CONTENTS

GREEK MYTHOLOGY

THE ODYSSEY – 13
ODYSSEUS IS A STONER – 26
THE ODYSSEY 2: THE TELEGONY – 27
IPHIGENIA – 29
(NOT) FUCKING CASSANDRA – 31
AGAMEMNON FUCKING DESERVED IT - 32
ARGONAUTS ASSEMBLE - 33
MEDEA FUCKS SHIT UP – 36
PENTHEUS HAS PROBLEMS WITH WOMEN – 39
HADES DOESN'T UNDERSTAND DATING – 40
MIDAS – 41
TAKING A JOYRIDE IN YOUR DAD'S WHEELS – 43
ARACHNE – 45
COCKBLOCKED BY A WALL - 46
PYGMALION – 47
PAN FUCKS EVERYTHING – 48
GANYMEDE – 49
OWLBEARS? - 50
ACTAEON – 51
EOS FUCKS GENDER ROLES – 52
CANNIBAL DINNER PARTIES SUCK – 53
CALLISTO – 54
ZEUS AND HERA – 55
AGDISTIS – 56
IXION IS A COMPLETE SHIT-BUCKET – 57
WINE OR POISON? – 58
MAGIC SNAKEY KISSES – 59
BLIND DATE – 60

LEANDER FORGETS HIS WATER-WINGS – 61
ECHO DON'T NEED NO MAN – 62
KING MINOS' SON GETS INTO A STICKY SITUATION – 63
ORION - 64

ROMAN MYTHOLOGY

THE AENEID – 67
CERES SETS A BABY ON FIRE – 80
FOX BONFIRE – 82

ENGLISH AND WELSH MYTHOLOGY

A SHITTY KNIGHT – 85
YOU CAN'T JUST FUCKING KILL BABY MERLIN – 86
MERLIN IS THE BEST WINGMAN – 87
ARTHUR GETS SOME DUMBSHIT SWORD – 88
ARTHUR'S INCEST ADVENTURE – 90
ARTHUR IS A CARELESS FUCK – 91
ARTHUR IS AN ASSHOLE TO CHILDREN – 92
MERLIN GETS A GIRLFRIEND – 93
FEAR FOR YOUR BEARD - 94
ARTHUR SAVES HIS CRAPPY BEARD – 95
SIR LAUNCELOT ENJOYS NAP TIME – 96
SURPRISE BABIES – 98
FLOWER FACE AND THE HOT KNIGHT – 99
SHITTY WELSH BOYFRIENDS – 101
DRAGONS IN A BLANKET – 102
A PLAGUE OF WIZARDS – 103

SCOTTISH MYTHOLOGY

ACTUAL CANNIBAL SEAN BEAN – 107
KELPIES DON'T KNOW SHIT ABOUT FIRE – 108
MICHAEL SCOTT STEALS SNAKE JUICE – 109
PASSIVE-AGGRESSIVE MERMAID – 110
THE GOODMAN O' WASTNESS IS REALLY A DICK – 111
FAIRIES WANT YOUR BABIES - 112

IRISH MYTHOLOGY

IRISH HEROES ARE UNPRONOUNCEABLE – 115
MOTHERFUCKING ARSON FAIRIES – 116
FIONN FUCKS A DEER – 117
HAIRY MONSTERS ARE FUCKING STUPID – 118
MORE CRAP CHILD-CARE – 119
DEATH RAY GIANTS – 120
EXPLODING BRAIN DEATH – 121
FUCKING UP THE WEDDING – 122
BRUTAL PUPPY MURDER – 123
OH SHIT, A PROPHECY – 124
CHILDREN ARE FUCKING TERRIFYING – 125
[OBLIGATORY TRAINING MONTAGE] – 126
CU CHULAINN FUCKS UP - 127
CU CHULAINN ADOPTS A WEIRD MUTANT INCEST BABY – 128
LITERAL PISSING CONTEST – 129
COW FIGHT! – 130
THE DEATH OF CU CHULAINN – 131

CHINESE MYTHOLOGY

BEGINNINGS: CHINESE STYLE – 135
WHERE DO (CHINESE) PEOPLE COME FROM? – 136
THE SKY IS FALLING – 137
MERCILESS DRAGON MURDER – 138
FUCKED-UP VAMPIRE DRAGONS – 139
HOW MANY EMPERORS HAVE YOU SEEN TODAY? – 140
THE RED EMPEROR IS METAL AS FUCK – 141
LIFEGUARDS? HA HA FUCK NO – 142
MAGICAL FOOT PREGNANCY – 143
XING TIAN THE HEADLESS GIANT – 144
FLAMING FIRE BABIES – 145
MURDERING BABIES – 146
HORSE+GIRL=WORST LOVE STORY EVER – 148

JAPANESE MYTHOLOGY

BEGINNINGS: AINU STYLE – 151
MEDICINE IS DANGEROUS – 152
ISLAND BABIES – 153
IZANAGI HAS ZOMBIE WIFE PROBLEMS – 154
TAIRA NO MASAKADO MURDERS EVERYONE – 156
KILLER FROG PRINCESS – 157
DEMONIC BUTT FONDLING – 158
DICKS ON PARADE – 159
PIRATES VS SNAILS – 160

FINNISH MYTHOLOGY

BEGINNINGS: FINNISH STYLE – 163
HOW DOES FARMING WORK? FIRE, THAT'S HOW – 164
RAP BATTLE WITH GANDALF – 166

A WIZARD'S KISS – 167
WIZARD HUNTING – 168
SANTA FUCKING LOVES PORRIDGE – 169

GREEK MYTHOLOGY

THE ODYSSEY: BOOK I

THE TROJAN WAR IS OVER. FUCKING FINALLY. TROY IS DESTROYED AND ALL THE INNOCENT PEOPLE IN IT ARE DEAD. ALL THE GREEKS HAVE GONE HOME. ODYSSEUS, HOWEVER, HAS BEEN KIDNAPPED BY A CRAZY BITCH CALLED CALYPSO, WHO HAS HIM STUCK IN A CAVE FOR SEX. FOR TEN YEARS.

ODYSSEUS SPENDS TEN ENTIRE YEARS STUCK ON AN ISLAND BEING FORCED TO SLEEP WITH A FUCKING CRAZY MAGIC LADY, AND HE'S UTTERLY FUCKING MISERABLE. LIFE IS SHIT FOR ODYSSEUS.

AFTER TEN YEARS, THE GODS SUDDENLY THINK "OH SHIT. WE FORGOT ABOUT ODYSSEUS." AND SET OUT TO HELP HIM. NATURALLY, THIS MEANS MAKING HIS LIFE EVEN SHITTIER.

ATHENA DRESSES UP AS A MAN, AND GOES TO TALK TO ODYSSEUS' SON TELEMACHUS, WHO'S FUCKING MISERABLE. HIS MUM'S SURROUNDED BY CREEPY GUYS AND HIS DAD HASN'T BEEN SEEN IN TEN YEARS. IT'S ALL A BIT SHIT.

ATHENA TELLS HIM TO GO ON A MAGICAL MYSTERY EXCITING VOYAGE, AND HE AGREES IN THE END. AND THEN EVERYONE'S MISERABLE ABOUT HOW SHITTY THEIR LIVES ARE FOR A BIT.

THE ODYSSEY: BOOK II

TELEMACHUS GETS UP, GOES TO SPEAK TO THE CREEPY SUITORS, TELLS THEM HIS LIFE IS SHIT, AND BURSTS INTO TEARS. EVERYONE JUST FUCKING STARES AT HIM. THEY'RE ALL DICKS; THEY MAKE ACHILLES LOOK LIKE A NICE AND BALANCED PERSON YOU MIGHT INVITE ROUND FOR DINNER.

THERE'S A FUCKING HUGE ARGUMENT, AND THEN TELEMACHUS AND ATHENA RUN AWAY TO SPARTA TOGETHER ON A SECRET DETECTIVE MISSION TO FIND OUT WHAT THE FUCK HAPPENED TO ODYSSEUS AND HOW HE'S SO LATE HOME.

EVERYONE ELSE'S FATHERS GOT HOME TEN YEARS AGO, AND HE'S STILL ON FUCKING MURDER-HOLIDAY.

THE ODYSSEY: BOOK III

TELEMACHUS AND ATHENA ARRIVE IN PYLOS, WHERE NESTOR LIVES. WHAT DO YOU THINK NESTOR DOES?

THAT'S RIGHT, HE TELLS A FUCKING STORY. HE'S NESTOR. HE NEVER DOES ANYTHING ELSE.

HE TELLS A STORY. IT'S SHIT. IT GOES ON FOR FUCKING AGES. THEN ATHENA TURNS INTO AN EAGLE AND FUCKS OFF.

THEN THEY HAVE A SACRIFICE, AND THEN TELEMACHUS HAS A BATH AND FUCKS OFF. NOBODY CAN STAND NESTOR.

THE ODYSSEY: BOOK IV

TELEMACHUS ARRIVES IN SPARTA, WHERE MENELAUS LIVES. THEN THEY HAVE YET ANOTHER FUCKING PARTY. AND THEN SOMEBODY MENTIONS TROY, AND EVERYONE BURSTS INTO FUCKING TEARS. IT'S A SHIT PARTY. HELEN GIVES EVERYONE DRUGS TO MAKE THEM HAPPY, AND IT GETS A LITTLE BIT LESS SHITTY.

THEN MENELAUS TELLS A STORY, AND TELEMACHUS FUCKS OFF TO THE NEXT PLACE ON HIS JOURNEY.

MEANWHILE, THE SUITORS PLOT TO MURDER TELEMACHUS. THEY'RE HORRIBLE SHITTY PEOPLE, AND IT MAKES PENELOPE CRY.

THE ODYSSEY: BOOK V

THE GODS FINALLY GET ROUND TO SENDING A MESSAGE TO CALYPSO TELLING HER TO STOP FUCKING WITH ODYSSEUS AND JUST LET HIM GO. TOOK THEM FUCKING LONG ENOUGH.

HERMES GOES TO CALYPSO'S ISLAND, WHERE ODYSSEUS IS STILL SITTING ON THE BEACH CRYING. AS HE HAS BEEN CONSTANTLY FOR SEVEN YEARS. HERMES TELLS CALYPSO TO LET ODYSSEUS GO, AND SHE SAYS HE'S JEALOUS AND TELLS HIM TO FUCK OFF, AND THEN GIVES IN AND LETS ODYSSEUS GO.

ODYSSEUS MAKES A RAFT, HOPS ON IT, AND DUTIFULLY FUCKS OFF BACK HOME TO PENELOPE.

POSEIDON SPOTS HIM ON THE WAY, THOUGH, AND MAKES A FUCKING MASSIVE STORM. THE RAFT IS SMASHED UP INTO FUCKING TINY PIECES. ODYSSEUS SPENDS TWO DAYS FLOATING IN THE WATER UNTIL HE EVENTUALLY WASHES UP ON A BEACH SOMEWHERE. HE FINDS A CAVE AND FALLS ASLEEP IN A PILE OF LEAVES, STILL PRETTY FUCKING MISERABLE. IT'S UNDERSTANDABLE, THOUGH, HIS LIFE IS SHIT.

THE ODYSSEY: BOOK VI

ODYSSEUS IS ASLEEP. ATHENA FUCKS OFF TO VISIT NAUSICAA, A PHAECIAN PRINCESS, AND SHOUTS AT HER FOR A BIT UNTIL SHE AGREES TO GO DOWN TO THE RIVER AND WASH HER CLOTHES. NAUSICAA PRESUMABLY SMELLS PRETTY FUCKING BAD.

NAUSICAA GOES DOWN TO THE RIVER TO WASH HER CLOTHES, MAKING FAR TOO MUCH FUCKING NOISE, AND ODYSSEUS WAKES UP. NAKED. HE GRABS A STICK TO COVER HIMSELF WITH, AND WANDERS OUT TO TALK TO ALL THE TEENAGE GIRLS PLAYING IN THE RIVER.

HE'S STILL NAKED. IT'S A FUCKING STICK. IT DOESN'T MAKE MUCH OF A DIFFERENCE.

ALL THE HANDMAIDS RUN AWAY, BECAUSE ODYSSEUS LOOKS LIKE A TRAMP. A NAKED TRAMP. NAUSICAA STAYS, THOUGH. SHE GIVES HIM CLOTHES AND FOOD AND TAKES HIM HOME, AND NOBODY THINKS IT'S WEIRD. AT LEAST HE'S NOT COMPLETELY FUCKING NAKED ANY MORE.

THE ODYSSEY: BOOK VII

ODYSSEUS GOES TO VISIT ALCINOUS, THE KING OF PHAEACIA. HE EXPLAINS WHAT'S HAPPENED, AND HOW HE MANAGED TO GET AWAY FROM CALYPSO. EVERYONE IS PRETTY FUCKING CONFUSED.

BOOK VII IS BASICALLY JUST A FUCKING RECAP. IT'S PRETTY SHIT.

THE ODYSSEY: BOOK VIII

ODYSSEUS GETS OUT OF BED AND GOES TO THE ASSEMBLY. THAT'S RIGHT, INSTEAD OF GOING HOME TO HIS WIFE HE FUCKS AROUND WITH POLITICS. IN THE END HE AND ALCINOUS PERSUADE THE PHAEACIANS TO LEND HIM A BOAT AND SOME MEN, AND HE CRIES. ODYSSEUS IS A WHINY LITTLE SHIT AND SPENDS A LOT OF TIME CRYING. GET FUCKING USED TO IT.

WHEN ODYSSEUS EVENTUALLY STOPS CRYING, THE PHAEACIANS ORGANISE SOME GAMES. ODYSSEUS ENTERS A FEW AND WINS EVERY SINGLE FUCKING ONE. EVERYONE GIVES HIM SHITLOADS OF PRESENTS, AND THEN THEY GO OFF FOR A PARTY. A BARD TELLS A STORY ABOUT THE END OF THE TROJAN WAR, AND ODYSSEUS BREAKS DOWN INTO FUCKING TEARS. AGAIN.

THE ODYSSEY: BOOK IX

ODYSSEUS STARTS TO EXPLAIN HOW HE GOT TO PHAEACIA. THAT'S RIGHT, MOTHERFUCKERS. IT'S FLASHBACK TIME.

ODYSSEUS AND HIS MEN GO TO ISMARUS AND KILL SHITLOADS OF PEOPLE. A FEW OF THE CREW DIE. EVERYONE CRIES.

THEN THEY GO TO THE LAND OF THE LOTUS-EATERS, AND ALL THE CREW GET HIGH AS FUCK AND WANT TO STAY BEHIND. ODYSSEUS SHOUTS AT THEM AND MAKES THEM ALL GET BACK ON THE FUCKING BOAT. EVERYONE CRIES. AGAIN.

THEN THEY GO TO THE ISLANDS WHERE THE CYCLOPES LIVE. THEY FIND A NICE CAVE WHERE A CYCLOPS LIVES, BRING A LOAD OF WINE AND SHIT LIKE THAT AS AN OFFERING, AND MOVE INTO THE CAVE WITHOUT FUCKING ASKING.

THE CYCLOPS COMES HOME TO FIND THAT ODYSSEUS AND HIS MEN HAVE EATEN HIS CHEESE, AND KILLS A FEW SAILORS. THEN HE EATS THEM. WHAT HAPPENS NEXT? THAT'S RIGHT. MORE FUCKING CRYING.

THE CYCLOPS GOES OUT IN THE MORNING, HAVING PROMISED TO EAT EVERYONE LATER, AND ODYSSEUS PLOTS TO BLIND HIM. THAT'S NOT FUCKING XENIA.

ODYSSEUS GETS OUT SHITLOADS OF WINE AND SHARPENS A STICK. POLYPHEMUS THE CYCLOPS DRINKS ALL THE WINE AND FALLS ASLEEP, AND ODYSSEUS STABS HIM IN THE FUCKING FACE WITH A POINTY STICK. NEEDLESS TO SAY, THE CYCLOPS IS PRETTY FUCKING FURIOUS, BUT HE'S NOW BLIND SO HE CAN'T REALLY DO MUCH.

IN THE MORNING, ODYSSEUS AND HIS MEN HIDE UNDER SOME SHEEP AND WAIT FOR THE CYCLOPS TO OPEN THE DOOR. WHEN HE OPENS THE DOOR, THEY SNEAK OFF UNDER THE SHEEP AND HOP IN THEIR BOAT. THE CYCLOPS WORKS OUT WHAT'S GOING ON, AND CHUCKS ROCKS AT THEM. FORTUNATELY FOR ODYSSEUS, THE CYCLOPS IS BLIND AND THEREFORE A FUCKING TERRIBLE SHOT, SO THEY ESCAPE UNHARMED.

THE ODYSSEY: BOOK X

ODYSSEUS AND HIS CREW GO TO VISIT AEOLUS, THE WIND GOD. AEOLUS LIVES ON A MOTHERFUCKING FLOATING ISLAND. THEY GET THERE AND AEOLUS STARTS A PARTY.

IT GOES ON FOR A WHOLE FUCKING MONTH.

AFTER A MONTH, HE GIVES ODYSSEUS A MAGIC BAG OF WIND. ODYSSEUS TAKES IT AND FUCKS OFF. THEY SAIL FOR NINE DAYS (THAT'S A WHOLE MONTH AND A BIT WITH NOBODY CRYING - PRETTY FUCKING GOOD GOING FOR ODYSSEUS).

SOME OF THE CREW START THINKING ODYSSEUS MIGHT HAVE GOLD IN THE BAG, BECAUSE ODYSSEUS IS A SHIT LEADER AND HASN'T TOLD THEM HE HAS A BAG OF MAGIC WIND. THEY WAIT TILL HE'S ASLEEP, THEN THEY SNEAK OVER AND OPEN THE BAG.

BIG FUCKING MISTAKE.

THE WIND RUSHES OUT AND BLOWS THEM ALL THE WAY BACK TO FUCKING AEOLUS. ODYSSEUS TELLS HIM HE NEEDS MORE WIND AND AEOLUS POINTS OUT ODYSSEUS IS A SHITTY LEADER AND TELLS HIM TO FUCK OFF.

THEY FUCK OFF AND GO TO VISIT THE LAISTRYGONIANS, WHO TURN OUT TO BE FUCKING MAN-EATING GIANTS. MOST OF THE CREW DIE, AND THE SURVIVORS SAIL ON TILL THEY REACH THE ISLAND OF CIRCE. ODYSSEUS SEES A HOUSE AND TELLS HIS MEN TO GO AND INVESTIGATE. THE MEN, REMEMBERING ALL THE AWFUL SHIT THAT'S HAPPENED BEFORE WHEN HE'S TOLD THEM TO VISIT HOUSES, BURST INTO FUCKING TEARS. AGAIN.

EURYLOCHUS AND TWENTY TWO OTHER MEN GO TO VISIT THE HOUSE, AND CIRCE TURNS THEM ALL EXCEPT EURYLOCHUS INTO FUCKING PIGS. THERE'S NO REASON WHY, SHE JUST DOES. EURYLOCHUS RUNS AWAY AND TELLS ODYSSEUS WHAT HAPPENED. IN TEARS. WHAT A FUCKING SURPRISE.

ODYSSEUS GOES TO VISIT CIRCE AND SLEEPS WITH HER UNTIL SHE AGREES TO TURN HIS MEN BACK INTO PEOPLE, BECAUSE SEX IS THE ONLY THING HE CAN THINK OF TO BE PERSUASIVE WITH.

ODYSSEUS GETS HOME TO FIND ALL HIS MEN IN TEARS BECAUSE THEY THINK HE'S DEAD. HE EXPLAINS WHAT'S HAPPENED AND THEY ALL MOVE IN WITH CIRCE. FOR AN ENTIRE FUCKING YEAR. ODYSSEUS ISN'T DOING WELL AT THIS GOING HOME SHIT AT ALL.

AFTER A YEAR, CIRCE TELLS ODYSSEUS TO FUCK OFF AND GO TO HADES. LITERALLY. HE HAS TO GO TO HADES AND TALK TO TIRESIAS.

ODYSSEUS PASSES THIS ON TO HIS MEN, AND WHAT HAPPENS? THAT'S RIGHT. MORE FUCKING TEARS.

THE ODYSSEY: BOOK XI

ODYSSEUS AND HIS MEN GET IN THEIR BOAT AND LEAVE CIRCE'S ISLAND. IN TEARS. AGAIN. THIS IS GETTING PRETTY FUCKING TEDIOUS.

THEY SAIL ALL THE WAY TO THE FUCKING EDGE OF THE WORLD, WHERE IT'S ALWAYS NIGHT AND EVERYONE THAT LIVES THERE THINKS IT'S SHIT. THEY STOP ON A BEACH, AND ODYSSEUS SACRIFICES A SHEEP. PRESUMABLY TIRESIAS LIKES LAMB.

FUCKLOADS OF GHOSTS SHOW UP FROM NOWHERE, AND ODYSSEUS THREATENS THEM ALL WITH A SWORD UNTIL TIRESIAS ARRIVES.

TIRESIAS TELLS ODYSSEUS NOT TO EAT THE MAGIC COWS AND THEN FUCKS OFF. UNSURPRISINGLY, TIRESIAS IS JUST AS FUCKING DIFFICULT AND ANNOYING AS HE WAS WHEN HE WAS STILL ALIVE.

THEN THE GHOST OF ODYSSEUS' MUM SHOWS UP AND HE TRIES TO HUG HER. IT DOESN'T WORK. SHE'S A FUCKING GHOST. SHE HAS TO EXPLAIN TO HIM THAT THAT'S NOT HOW GHOSTS FUCKING WORK, AND HE'S NOT HAPPY. HE DOESN'T CRY THOUGH (FOR ONCE).

ODYSSEUS SEES MORE GHOSTS. EVERY SINGLE FUCKING ONE IS LISTED. IT'S A BIT LIKE BOOK II OF THE ILIAD AND THE FUCKING CATALOGUE OF SHIPS. IN THE END AGAMEMNON SHOWS UP AND EXPLAINS TO ODYSSEUS THAT EVERYTHING IS SHIT AND HE WAS MURDERED BY HIS OWN FUCKING WIFE. HE GIVES A BIT OF BULLSHIT ADVICE ABOUT WHAT TO DO WHEN ODYSSEUS GETS HOME, AND THEN THEY BOTH BURST INTO TEARS. THIS IS GETTING FUCKING RIDICULOUS.

ACHILLES ARRIVES A BIT LATER TO FIND THEM STILL CRYING ON THE FLOOR AND ASKS FOR NEWS OF HIS SON. BECAUSE

ACHILLES IS A DICK HE DOESN'T OFFER ODYSSEUS ANY ADVICE OR ANYTHING, AND JUST FUCKS OFF WITHOUT HELPING.

IN THE END ODYSSEUS GETS BORED OF TALKING TO YET MORE FUCKING GHOSTS AND FUCKS OFF BACK TO HIS SHIP.

THE ODYSSEY: BOOK XII

ODYSSEUS AND HIS MEN SAIL BACK TO CIRCE'S ISLAND, AND SHE WARNS THEM ABOUT ALL THE HORRIBLE FUCKING MONSTERS THEY'RE GOING TO HAVE TO DEAL WITH. THEN THEY LEAVE, THIS TIME WITHOUT CRYING AT ALL.

SOON THEY REACH THE ISLAND OF THE SIRENS, MAGIC MAN-EATING LADIES THAT SING. THEY'RE PRETTY FUCKING SCARY. ODYSSEUS MAKES ALL HIS MEN SHOVE WAX IN THEIR EARS SO THEY CAN'T HEAR THE SINGING, AND MAKES THEM TIE HIM TO THE MAST BECAUSE HE'S FUCKING STUPID AND WANTS TO HEAR IT. IT'S NOT ALL THAT GREAT. THEY KEEP SAILING ON.

THEN ODYSSEUS SEES A WAVE. IT'S MOTHERFUCKING CHARYBDIS THE WHIRLPOOL MONSTER. HE TELLS THE MEN TO AVOID IT, CONVENIENTLY NOT WARNING THEM ABOUT THE MANY-HEADED MONSTER SCYLLA ON THE OTHER SIDE. ODYSSEUS IS A SHIT LEADER. SCYLLA EATS SIX MEN. ODYSSEUS DOESN'T GIVE A SHIT. IN THE END THEY ESCAPE, AND LAND ON THE ISLAND OF THE FUCKING SUN GOD.

ODYSSEUS REMEMBERS WHAT TIRESIAS AND CIRCE TOLD HIM ABOUT THE FUCKING MAGIC SUN COWS AND TELLS HIS MEN TO AVOID THE ISLAND. THEY'RE ALL TIRED AND HUNGRY AND LAST TIME HE TOLD THEM TO DO SOMETHING SIX OF THEM GOT FUCKING EATEN, SO THEY IGNORE HIM AND LAND ANYWAY.

THEN THE WIND JUST FUCKING STOPS. THEY CAN'T LEAVE THE ISLAND.

AFTER A WHOLE FUCKING MONTH, THE MEN ARE PRETTY HUNGRY. THEY IGNORE ODYSSEUS' ORDERS AND EAT THE FUCKING MAGIC COWS. THEY CAN TELL THIS IS A BAD IDEA

BECAUSE WHEN THEY COOK THE BEEF IT MOOS. NORMAL BEEF DOES NOT FUCKING MOO.

IN THE END THE WIND PICKS UP AGAIN SO THEY LEAVE. AT THIS POINT, THE GODS GO "HA HA FUCK YOU" AND MAKE A FUCKING MASSIVE STORM. THE SHIP GETS BLOWN TO BITS AND ODYSSEUS GETS WASHED UP ON CALYPSO'S ISLAND.

AND THAT'S THE END OF THE FUCKING FLASHBACK.

THE ODYSSEY: BOOK XIII

ALCINOUS TELLS ODYSSEUS HE'S SURE HE'LL GET HOME WITH NO MORE PROBLEMS, AND THEN FUCKING FORCES ALL HIS FRIENDS TO GIVE ODYSSEUS MORE PRESENTS. ODYSSEUS TAKES THE PRESENTS AND FUCKS OFF.

ODYSSEUS SAILS BACK TO ITHAKA SAFELY AND HIDES ALL HIS NEW TREASURE HE GOT FROM ALCINOUS UNDER A TREE BECAUSE HE'S AFRAID SOMEBODY MIGHT FUCKING STEAL IT. THEN HE GOES TO SLEEP.

WHEN HE WAKES UP EVERYTHING LOOKS DIFFERENT BECAUSE HE HASN'T BEEN HOME IN YEARS. ODYSSEUS IS A FUCKING IDIOT, SO HE THINKS HE'S SOMEWHERE COMPLETELY DIFFERENT AND BURSTS INTO FUCKING TEARS AGAIN.

ATHENA SHOWS UP AND TELLS HIM HE'S BEING FUCKING STUPID AND HE STOPS CRYING. THEN SHE TELLS HIM TO MURDER ALL OF PENELOPE'S FUCKING SUITORS AND DISGUISES HIM AS AN OLD MAN.

THE ODYSSEY: BOOK XIV

ODYSSEUS, STILL DISGUISED AS AN OLD MAN, GOES TO VISIT HIS PIG COLLECTION. ODYSSEUS' PIG COLLECTION IS FUCKING INSANE. HE HAS 360 FUCKING PIGS. THAT'S A FUCKLOAD OF PIGS. ONE OF THE SWINEHERDS GIVES HIM FOOD AND TELLS HIM HOW SHIT EVERYTHING IS, AND ODYSSEUS MAKES UP SOME

COMPLETE BULLSHIT AND TELLS HIM A COMPLETELY MADE UP LIFE STORY. IT'S ALL A BIT FUCKING POINTLESS.

THE ODYSSEY: BOOK XV

ATHENA GOES TO SPARTA AND TELLS TELEMACHUS TO FUCK OFF BACK TO ITHAKA. MENELAUS GIVES HIM A HUGE PILE OF PRESENTS AND THEN HE DUTIFULLY FUCKS OFF HOME. MEANWHILE, ODYSSEUS IS STILL MERCILESSLY FUCKING BULLYING THE POOR SWINEHERD TO SEE IF HE'S TRUSTWORTHY. ODYSSEUS IS A FUCKING AWFUL PERSON.

THE ODYSSEY: BOOK XVI

ODYSSEUS GETS UP IN THE MORNING (STILL DISGUISED AS AN OLD MAN) TO FIND THAT HIS SON TELEMACHUS HAS COME TO VISIT THE SWINEHERD. TELEMACHUS IS STILL MISERABLE BECAUSE HE THINKS HIS DAD'S DEAD, BUT BECAUSE ODYSSEUS IS A SHIT FATHER HE KEEPS PRETENDING TO BE AN OLD MAN FOR SOME FUCKING SADISTIC REASON.

TELEMACHUS AGREES TO TAKE ODYSSEUS BACK TO THE PALACE, AND THEN ATHENA SHOWS UP AND TELLS ODYSSEUS TO STOP BEING SUCH A FUCKING DICK AND ADMIT TO WHO HE IS.

ODYSSEUS TELLS TELEMACHUS WHO HE IS AND TELEMACHUS TELLS HIM TO FUCK OFF AND STOP LYING. ODYSSEUS TELLS HIM AGAIN AND THEN THEY BOTH SIT ON THE FLOOR AND JUST FUCKING CRY.

ODYSSEUS AND TELEMACHUS COME UP WITH A PLOT TO MURDER ALL THE SUITORS AND THEN THEY GO BACK TO THE PALACE TO FUCKING KILL PEOPLE.

THE ODYSSEY: BOOK XVII

TELEMACHUS TELLS HIS MUM WHAT HE'S BEEN DOING WHILE AWAY, AND THEN THEY HAVE A FUCKING MASSIVE PARTY. SHE STILL HAS NO IDEA ODYSSEUS IS EVEN FUCKING ALIVE THOUGH, SO SHE'S STILL FUCKING MISERABLE.

ODYSSEUS HEADS TO THE PALACE, AND ONE OF HIS DOGS SEES HIM ON THE WAY. THE DOG IS SO FUCKING EXCITED TO SEE HIM THAT IT DIES.

ODYSSEUS FUCKING CRIES. AGAIN.

THEN HE GOES INTO THE HOUSE, AND ALL THE SUITORS LAUGH AT HIM AND THROW STUFF AND HIT HIM BECAUSE HE'S STILL DRESSED LIKE A FUCKING TRAMP FOR NO GOOD REASON.

THE ODYSSEY: BOOK XVIII

THE SUITORS FIND ANOTHER TRAMP AND MAKE HIM FIGHT ODYSSEUS FOR FOOD. NOBODY IN THIS FUCKING POEM UNDERSTANDS HOW XENIA WORKS.

ODYSSEUS BEATS THE SHIT OUT OF THE OTHER TRAMP AND THE SUITORS ARE IMPRESSED. PENELOPE COMES DOWNSTAIRS AND TELLS TELEMACHUS HE'S A SHIT SON. THE SUITORS LAUGH AT EVERYONE. IT'S ALL FUCKING HORRIBLE.

THE ODYSSEY: BOOK XIX

PENELOPE ASKS ODYSSEUS WHO HE IS AND WHERE HE'S FROM AND, BECAUSE HE'S A DICK, HE REFUSES TO REVEAL HIMSELF AND JUST MAKES UP YET MORE FUCKING BULLSHIT.

THEN PENELOPE GETS ODYSSEUS' OLD NURSE TO COME AND WASH HIS FEET. SHE RECOGNISES HIM BY HIS FUCKING FEET AND HE HAS TO TELL HER TO SHUT THE FUCK UP.

THEN EVERYONE GOES TO BED. PENELOPE CRIES A LOT AND ODYSSEUS JUST PLOTS FUCKING MURDER.

THE ODYSSEY: BOOK XX

ODYSSEUS SLEEPS. PENELOPE DOESN'T SLEEP - SHE JUST FUCKING CRIES INSTEAD.

AT DINNER, THE SUITORS THROW FOOD AT ODYSSEUS. HE DOESN'T REACT. HE JUST SMILES. HE KNOWS IT'S NEARLY FUCKING MURDER TIME.

THE ODYSSEY: BOOK XXI

PENELOPE DECIDES SHE'S HAD ENOUGH OF THIS BULLSHIT AND THAT IT'S TIME TO START A FUCKING COMPETITION. SHE GETS ODYSSEUS' BOW AND TELLS THE SUITORS TO FIRE AN ARROW THROUGH THE HANDLES OF TWELVE FUCKING AXES.

NONE OF THEM CAN DO IT AT ALL. THEN ODYSSEUS TAKES THE BOW AND FIRES, AND THE ARROW GOES ALL THE WAY THROUGH ALL TWELVE AXES AND RIGHT OUT THE FUCKING DOOR. EVERYONE STARES AT HIM.

THE ODYSSEY: BOOK XXII

ODYSSEUS THROWS OFF HIS DISGUISE, SHOUTS "HAHA! FUCK YOU ALL! I'M MOTHERFUCKING ODYSSEUS, BITCHES!" AND SHOOTS ALL THE FUCKING SUITORS IN THE FACE. THERE'S BLOOD ALL OVER THE FUCKING FLOOR. TWENTY YEARS AWAY, AND HE THINKS THE BEST WAY TO COME HOME IS TO LIE TO HIS FAMILY FOR A WEEK AND THEN MURDER ALL THE FUCKING GUESTS.

ODYSSEUS DOESN'T UNDERSTAND FUCKING XENIA EITHER.

THE ODYSSEY: BOOK XXIII

THE OLD NURSE RUNS UPSTAIRS TO TELL PENELOPE THAT ODYSSEUS JUST CAME HOME AND MURDERED ALL THE FUCKING SUITORS. PENELOPE TELLS HER TO FUCK OFF AND

STOP MAKING UP BULLSHIT. IN THE END SHE AGREES TO COME DOWNSTAIRS AND HAVE A LOOK.

SHE SEES ODYSSEUS STANDING IN THE MIDDLE OF ALL THE FUCKING CARNAGE AND TELLS HIM SHE'LL GET THE BED BROUGHT DOWN.

ODYSSEUS DROPS HIS BOW AND TELLS HER TO FUCK OFF. HE BUILT THAT BED ROUND A WHOLE FUCKING TREE, AND SOMETHING IS CLEARLY WRONG.

HE'S FALLEN RIGHT INTO HER FUCKING TRAP. NOW SHE KNOWS IT'S REALLY HIM SHE HUGS HIM AND THEN THEY BOTH CRY FOR FUCKING AGES.

AFTER THEY'VE RECOVERED AND ODYSSEUS HAS TOLD THE STORY OF WHAT HAPPENED WHILE HE WAS AWAY, ODYSSEUS AND TELEMACHUS PUT ON THEIR ARMOUR AND SNEAK OUT OF THE HOUSE.

THE ODYSSEY: BOOK XXIV

THE GHOSTS OF THE SUITORS ALL GO DOWN TO HADES AND TELL THE DEAD GREEK HEROES WHAT THE FUCK HAPPENED TO THEM.

MEANWHILE, ODYSSEUS AND TELEMACHUS GO TO VISIT ODYSSEU'S DAD LAERTES. ODYSSEUS SAYS HI TO LAERTES AND TELLS HIM WHO HE IS. LAERTES TELLS HIM TO FUCK OFF AND STOP LYING. THIS IS A RECURRING THEME. IN THE END ODYSSEUS CONVINCES HIS DAD IT'S REALLY HIM, AND THEY HAVE A FUCKING MASSIVE PARTY.

THAT'S THE END. IT'S A HAPPIER ENDING THAN THE FUCKING ILIAD.

ODYSSEUS IS A STONER

FURTHER EVIDENCE THAT ODYSSEUS IS A COMPLETE SHIT-WEASEL.

PALAMEDES IS THE FUCKER WHO TRICKED ODYSSEUS INTO JOINING THE TROJAN WAR BY PUTTING HIS BABY UNDER A PLOUGH. THAT SOUNDS LIKE A DICK MOVE, BUT ODYSSEUS WAS PRETENDING TO BE CRAZY TO GET OUT OF A PROMISE HE'D MADE, BECAUSE HE'S A SLIMY DICK.

ODYSSEUS WAS STILL BITTER ABOUT THIS DURING THE WAR, SO HE HIDES GOLD IN PALAMEDES' TENT AND SETS UP SOME SHIT WITH AN INCRIMINATING LETTER AND ACCUSES PALAMEDES OF SIDING WITH THE TROJANS. EVERYONE BELIEVES ODYSSEUS BECAUSE HE'S SNEAKY AS FUCK, AND PALAMEDES IS STONED TO DEATH, BECAUSE ANYTHING ELSE WOULD BE WAY TOO BORING.

BACK HOME, PALAMEDES' DAD NAUPLIUS HEARS ABOUT THIS FUCKERY AND GOES TO TROY TO INVESTIGATE HIS SON'S DEATH. AGAMEMNON HASN'T GOT TIME FOR THAT SHIT AND BELIEVES THE CRAP ODYSSEUS WAS SAYING.

IN REVENGE, NAUPLIUS DOES SOME FUCKERY WITH BEACONS THAT CAUSES SOME OF THE GREEKS TO SHIPWRECK ON THEIR WAY HOME, AND ALSO TELLS THEIR WIVES TO SLEEP AROUND WHILE THE MEN ARE AT TROY. CREATIVE, MOST FOLKS JUST GO WITH STAB-BASED REVENGE.

THE ODYSSEY 2: THE TELEGONY

TIME FOR SOME SHITTY ODYSSEY FAN-FICTION/SEQUEL, ATTRIBUTED TO SOME FUCKER CALLED EUGAMON (OR SOME OTHER FUCKERS), AND SADLY NOW LOST.

SO YOU FUCKERS KNOW ODYSSEUS HAD THIS LONG LIST OF THINGS TO DO THAT TIRESIAS MENTIONED IN FUCKING BOOK XI? LIKE GO BE NICE TO POSEIDON AND BURY A FUCKING OAR? WELL ODYSSEUS FUCKS OFF TO THESPROTIA TO GET THAT SHIT DONE. THESPROTIA HAS A HOT QUEEN, KALLIDIKE, SO NATURALLY ODYSSEUS HAS TO FUCK HER.

THEY HAVE A SON, POLYPOITES, WHO DOESN'T REALLY DO MUCH, AND EVENTUALLY ODYSSEUS (WHO MUST BE SUPER FUCKING OLD BY NOW) HELPS THESPROTIA IN A WAR. KALLIDIKE IS KILLED, SO ODYSSEUS FUCKS BACK TO ITHACA.

MEANWHILE OTHER, MORE INTERESTING SHIT IS GOING DOWN. REMEMBER WHEN ODYSSEUS HAD A THING WITH WITCH-BITCH CIRCE FOR A YEAR (WHEN HE WAS SUPPOSED TO BE GETTING BACK TO HIS ACTUAL WIFE, WHAT AN ASSHOLE)? WELL SHE GOT PREGNANT AND HAD SOME ICKY BABY, TELEGONOS. THE KID GROWS UP AND ATHENA THINKS IT WOULD BE A GREAT IDEA FOR CIRCE TO TELL HIM ABOUT HIS FATHER.

TELEGONOS FUCKS OFF TO LOOK FOR HIS DADDY, ARMED WITH SOME RAD-ASS SPEAR MADE WITH A STING-RAY'S MOTHERFUCKING STING. HE ENDS UP IN A STORM (LIKE EVERY OTHER FUCKER) AND WASHES UP IN ITHACA, BUT HE DOESN'T KNOW THAT. TELEGONOS THEN TAKES THE LOGICAL DECISION - WHEN IN FOREIGN LAND, BE A FUCKING PIRATE. SO HE STARTS STEALING SHIT AND BEATING PEOPLE UP, NOT KNOWING WHERE HE IS.

ODYSSEUS COMES OUT TO DEFEND HIS LAND, AND TELEGONOS ENDS UP KILLING HIM. AWKWARD. AS HE LIES THERE DYING, THEY SUDDENLY RECOGNISE EACH OTHER, AND TELEGONOS REALISES HE'S FUCKED UP.

TELEGONOS TAKES ODYSSEUS' BODY, AS WELL AS PENELOPE AND TELEMACHUS (FOR NO APPARENT REASON) BACK TO

AEAEA, WHERE HIS MUMMY CIRCE LIVES. THEY BURY ODYSSEUS THERE AND CIRCE TRIES TO FIX SHIT BY MAKING TELEGONOS, TELEMACHUS AND PENELOPE IMMORTAL. THEN TELEGONOS MARRIES PENELOPE AND TELEMACHUS MARRIES CIRCE IN SOME STRANGE STEP-MOTHER/SON FUCKERY.

PRETENTIOUS MOVIE CRITIC VOICE WE PREFERRED THE ORIGINAL.

IPHIGENIA

TEAM GREECE ARE HELLA PSYCHED TO GO AND BEAT UP SOME TROJANS, BECAUSE MENELAUS WANTS HIS DAMN WIFE BACK.

THE ARMIES ARE ALL GATHERED AND THEY'VE FINALLY STOPPED ODYSSEUS FROM PRETENDING TO BE FUCKING CRAZY TO SKIP OUT OF GOING. HE WAS FUCKING AROUND WITH HIS PLOUGH (BEING CRAZY), BUT HE STOPPED THIS SHIT WHEN SOME DICK PUT HIS BABY SON IN FRONT OF THE PLOUGH. EVENTUALLY ODYSSEUS FUCKS OFF TO JOIN THE WE-HATE-THE-TROJANS GANG.

THE GREEK FUCKERS GET AS FAR AS AULIS. THEN SOMEONE FUCKS UP AND ARTEMIS GETS OFFENDED, AND STOPS ALL THE WINDS AND SAILING THINGS. EITHER SOME BITCH KILLED A PREGNANT BUNNY, OR AGAMEMNON BRAGGED ABOUT BEING A BOSS-ASS HUNTER; EITHER WAY LADY ARTEMIS WAS FUCKING MAD.

THE ONLY WAY TO APPEASE HER, ACCORDING TO A TRIPPY SEER, IS FOR AGAMEMNON TO SACRIFICE HIS DAUGHTER, IPHIGENIA. OH SNAP.

SINCE EVERYONE IS READY AND EXCITED FOR BEATING THE SHIT OUT OF TROJANS, THEY CAN'T TURN BACK. MENELAUS TELLS HIS BRO AGAMEMNON THAT HE MUST DO THE THING, EVEN THOUGH IT'S PRETTY SHITTY.

SO THEY SEND FOR IPHIGENIA. IT'S REALLY FUCKING AWKWARD, BECAUSE IT'S SET UP AS A WEDDING BETWEEN HER AND ACHILLES AND SHE'S REALLY FUCKING HAPPY ABOUT IT, BUT DADDY KNOWS WHAT SHIT IS ABOUT TO GO DOWN.

EVENTUALLY IPHIGENIA AND ACHILLES FIND OUT WHAT THE FUCK WAS GOING ON. INITIALLY ACHILLES GETS MAD AND WANTS TO STAB A BITCH AND IPHIGENIA AND HER MUM CLYTEMNESTRA ARE UNDERSTANDABLY NOT HAPPY ABOUT THE HUMAN SACRIFICE SITUATION.

BUT THEN IPHIGENIA DECIDES TO BE A BRAVE LITTLE FUCKER, AND GOES OFF TO BE SACRIFICED VOLUNTARILY. JUST AS SHE'S

ABOUT TO BE KILLED, ARTEMIS GETS HER SHIT TOGETHER AND TELEPORTS IPHIGENIA OUT OF THAT FUCKERY, SWAPPING HER WITH A DOE.

IPHIGENIA GETS DUMPED IN TAURIS WHERE SHE GOES ON TO DO SOME PRIESTESS FUCKERY, AND THE GREEKS SAIL OFF TO FUCK TROY. EVERYBODY WINS ~~(EXCEPT THE TROJANS)~~.

(NOT) FUCKING CASSANDRA

THIS CRAZY LADY IS THE DAUGHTER OF PRIAM AND HECUBA, SO EFFECTIVELY A DISNEY PRINCESS OF THE MYTHOLOGICAL WORLD. SHE'S REALLY FUCKING HOT, AND APOLLO WANTS TO SLEEP WITH HER.

GOOD-GUY APOLLO WANTS SOME CONSENT, WHICH WAS FUCKING NICE OF BY GREEK GOD STANDARDS. SO HE GIVES HER A PRESENT TO PERSUADE HER. HE GIVES HER THE GIFT OF PROPHECY, NOT JUST FUCKING FLOWERS OR SOME SHIT LIKE THAT.

BUT CASSANDRA SAYS "FUCK NO, BITCH", AND APOLLO GETS PRETTY MAD ABOUT THIS. BUT HE CAN'T TAKE BACK HIS GIFT. HE JUST MAKES IT GO BAD, SO CASSANDRA KNOWS ALL THIS PROPHECY SHIT BUT NOBODY BELIEVES HER. SHE THEN BECOMES TROY'S OFFICIAL CRAZY LADY, AND SHOUTS IMPORTANT SOUNDING CRAP ALL THE TIME.

ALTERNATIVELY SHE GOT THE PROPHECY CRAP FROM WHEN SHE FELL ASLEEP IN A TEMPLE AND SOME SNAKES JUST FUCKING LICKED HER EARS. TRIPPY SHIT.

AFTER TROY GETS DESTROYED, THE TOTAL DICKBAG SHITFACE LESSER AJAX DRAGS HER OFF AND RAPES HER (ATHENA THEN KILLS THE FUCK OUT OF HIM LATER, DON'T WORRY), AND SHE'S THEN GIVEN TO CHIEF-ASSHOLE AGAMEMNON AS A CONCUBINE.

AGAMEMNON FUCKING DESERVED IT

AGAMEMNON RETURNS HOME FROM TROY WITH CASSANDRA AS HIS NEW LADY-FRIEND. HIS WIFE CLYTEMNESTRA IS NATURALLY SERIOUSLY FUCKING MAD ABOUT THIS, PROBABLY BECAUSE HE'S ALSO TAKEN 10 YEARS TO BEAT UP TROY AND HAS ALSO SACRIFICED THEIR LITTLE DAUGHTER IPHIGENIA.

BUT THEN AGAIN CLYTEMNESTRA HAS ALSO BEEN CHEATING ON AGAMEMNON, WITH AEGISTHUS, AND DOING LOTS OF FUCKING NON-WOMANLY THINGS LIKE MAKING DECISIONS AND RULING OVER SHIT WHILE HER HUSBAND WAS AWAY.

AGAMEMNON DOESN'T SEEM TO REALISE CLYTEMNESTRA WOULD BE MAD WITH HIM, SO HE JUST FUCKING STROLLS IN WITH CASSANDRA ON HIS ARM. CASSANDRA SUDDENLY FREAKS THE FUCK OUT ABOUT MURDER AND PLOTS AND SHIT, BUT NOBODY GIVES A FUCK BECAUSE THEY THINK SHE'S JUST CRAZY.

AS ALWAYS, SHE IS RIGHT AND CLYTEMNESTRA AND AEGISTHUS THEN BRUTALLY MURDER BOTH CASSANDRA AND AGAMEMNON - EITHER IN THE BATH TUB, WITH A CLOAK OR AT A FEAST. WHO KNOWS. MYTHS CAN BE LIKE FUCKING CLUEDO SOMETIMES.

ARGONAUTS ASSEMBLE

THE SHIT IS GOING DOWN IN THESSALY. THE THRONE HAS JUST BEEN FUCKING TAKEN, AND THE NEW ASSHOLE KING PELIAS WANTS EVERY POSSIBLE RISK TO HIS THRONE KILLED. THIS INCLUDES HIS UGLY-ASS NEW-BORN NEPHEW, JASON. LUCKILY HIS MOTHER JUST PRETENDS HE'S FUCKING DEAD AND SMUGGLES HIM OUT TO MOUNT PELION, TO BE BROUGHT UP BY A FUCKING CENTAUR (CHIRON). RESPONSIBLE PARENTING RIGHT THERE.

FINALLY WHEN JASON GETS BIG AND MORE OF A DICK HE RETURNS TO HIS HOME CITY, BUT SNEAKILY DISGUISED. UNCLE PELIAS STILL FUCKING RECOGNISES HIM BECAUSE HIS CLEVER DISGUISE SUCKS. HE DOESN'T MAKE IT OBVIOUS THOUGH, AND ASKS JASON WHAT THE FUCK HE WOULD DO IF AN ORACLE SAID SOMEONE WAS GOING TO KILL YOU. JASON THEN JUST GIVES THE VAGUEST FUCKING ANSWER EVER AND SAYS HE WOULD SEND HIM TO GO AND GET A GOLDEN FUCKING FLEECE. HERA MADE HIM SAY THIS SHIT, BUT IT STILL SOUNDS PRETTY FUCKING RANDOM.

BASICALLY AFTER A CONVOLUTED GHOST-BASED SUB-PLOT (YES THIS IS VERY FUCKING HAMLET), PELIAS ENDS UP SAYING THAT JASON CAN HAVE THE THRONE, BUT ONLY IF HE CAN BRING BACK THIS SHINY-ASS FLEECE FROM THE SCARY LAND OF COLCHIS GUARDED BY A HUGE-ASS DRAGON. BASICALLY PELIAS SAYS FUCK OFF AND DIE.

BUT JASON DOESN'T WANT TO GO ALONE. SO HE ASSEMBLES A TEAM OF EARTH'S MIGHTIEST HEROES. THESE FUCKING INCLUDE: HERACLES, BELLEROPHON, ATALANTA, CAENEUS, NESTOR (WE PRESUME HE'S FUCKING OLD AND REPETITIVE ALREADY BY THIS POINT), THESEUS, CASTOR, POLLUX AND BASICALLY FUCKING EVERY HERO EVER. TONNES OF DICKS IN A BOAT, BASICALLY.

THE ROSTER ALSO INCLUDES A FUCKER CALLED BUTES, WHO IS RESIDENT BEE-KEEPER. HE DOESN'T REALLY FUCKING DO ANYTHING ON THE EPIC VOYAGE EXCEPT FUCK OFF AND FUCK APHRODITE.

THE WEIRDEST THING ABOUT THE ENTIRE AFFAIR IS HOW HERA FAVOURS JASON, BECAUSE HERA REALLY FUCKING HATES EVERYONE.

JASON AND HIS GANG HAVE A PRETTY SHITTY JOURNEY TO COLCHIS, INVOLVING CRAZY HORNY WARRIOR LADIES, AND A WEDDING CRASHED BY GIANTS WITH SIX FUCKING HANDS. THERE'S ALSO A MOMENT WHERE HERACLES LOSES HIS BOYFRIEND HYLAS, AND GOES OFF TO LOOK FOR HIM, THEN JUST DOESN'T FUCKING COME BACK. ASSHOLE.

EVENTUALLY THEY GET TO COLCHIS, AND EVERYONE FUCKS RIGHT UP TO THE PALACE, NO SNEAKINESS AT ALL. KING AEETES IS INSIDE WITH HIS CREEPY-ASS WITCH DAUGHTER MEDEA. JASON ASKS NICELY FOR THE GOLDEN FLEECE, AND IS TOLD TO JUST FUCK RIGHT OFF. THEN HE CHANGES HIS MIND AND JUST TELLS JASON SURE, AS LONG AS HE FUCKING PLOUGHS A FIELD WITH FUCKING FIRE BULLS THEN PLANTS SOME DRAGON'S TEETH IN THE EARTH. JASON IS RATHER FUCKING SURPRISED AT THIS, WHICH IS WEIRD BECAUSE THIS KIND OF SHIT HAPPENS A LOT IN MYTHICAL GREECE.

AT THIS POINT THE GODS DECIDE TO REALLY FUCKING MIX SHIT UP BY MAKING MEDEA FALL MADLY IN LOVE WITH JASON. SHE OFFERS JASON HELP WITH ALL THIS SHIT, SO LONG AS HE SWEARS TO BE HER HUSBAND. HE SWEARS TO LOVE HER FOR EVER AND EVER AND EVER (REMEMBER THIS BIT FOR LATER, MOTHERFUCKERS). SHE THEN GIVES HIM A SHIT-TONNE OF MAGICAL POTION CRAP, SO HE PASSES THE FUCKING CHALLENGE.

KING AEETES IS A SELFISH DICK AND WANTS TO KEEP HIS SHINY FUCKING SHEEP, AND PLOTS TO KILL JASON AND HIS GANG. MEDEA ISN'T FUCKING HAVING THIS SO AGAIN SHE HELPS JASON BY SHOWING HIM TO THE FLEECE AND THEN KNOCKING THE FUCKING GUARD-DRAGON UNCONSCIOUS WITH SOME DRUGS.

JASON GRABS THE FUCKING FLEECE, AND FUCKS BACK TO THESSALY. HOWEVER, MEDEA MAKES THIS A WHOLE LOAD MORE FUN BY KILLING HER HALF-BROTHER AND CUTTING HIM

INTO TINY FUCKING PIECES. JASON THEN HAS TO LICK UP SOME OF THE BLOOD TO STOP THE GHOST FUCKING HAUNTING THEM. THEY SHOULD DO THIS SHIT IN GHOST-BUSTERS. THIS SLOWS DOWN AEETES FROM COMING AFTER THEM AS HE'S TOO BUSY PICKING UP BITS OF HIS SON. LOVELY.

MEDEA FUCKS SHIT UP

THE ARGONAUTS GET HOME WITH THE FLEECE AND EVERYTHING IS GREAT. EXCEPT JASON'S PARENTS AND NEW-BORN BROTHER HAVE ALL BEEN FUCKING SLAUGHTERED BY KING PELIAS. FUCK. JASON KEEPS A LOW PROFILE FOR A BIT AND LETS MEDEA SNEAK INTO THE PALACE. BY SNEAK WE MEAN SHOUTING CRAZILY ABOUT HOW ARTEMIS WAS FLYING INTO THE CITY ON A FUCKING SNAKE CHARIOT.

EVERYONE PANICS AND PELIAS ASKS MEDEA WHAT THE FUCK HE SHOULD DO, BECAUSE SHE SEEMS LIKE A REASONABLE FUCKER TO ASK. SHE'S NOT. IT'S A FUCKING LIE. MEDEA TELLS HIM HE SHOULD SHOW HIS FUCKING FAITH BY TURNING HIMSELF INTO A YOUNG MAN. SHE SHOWS HIM BY CUTTING UP SOME OLD SHEEP AND PUTTING IT ON LOW BOIL FOR AROUND 20 MINUTES, ADDING HERBS AND MUTTERING INCANTATIONS OCCASIONALLY. THIS MAGICALLY TURNS IT INTO A CUTE LITTLE LAMB. IT'S ALL A FUCKING LIE. MEDEA FUCKING LIES A LOT.

MEDEA THEN CONVINCES PELIAS' DAUGHTERS TO CUT HIM UP AND PUT HIM IN THE CAULDRON, AND HE JUST LIES THERE AND LETS THEM FUCKING DO IT. PELIAS DIES REALLY FUCKING HORRIBLY, AND DOESN'T TURN INTO A FUCKING LAMB. NOT ENOUGH FUCKING HERBS, CLEARLY.

PEOPLE DON'T FUCKING LIKE IT WHEN YOU MURDER THEIR KING, SO JASON AND MEDEA GET THE FUCK OUT OF TOWN. THEY GO TO CORINTH AND HAVE SOME LOVELY FUCKING CHILDREN. EVERYTHING IS HAPPY. BUT JASON IS SERIOUSLY FUCKING SUSPICIOUS OF CREEPY-ASS MEDEA AND TAKES THE OPPORTUNITY TO DUMP HER AND GET ENGAGED TO GLAUKE, THE DAUGHTER OF THE KING OF CORINTH, CREON (NOT THE FUCKER FROM THEBES, THOUGH THEY WERE PROBABLY BUDDIES IN ASSHOLERY).

AS SHE IS A BARBARIAN AND FUCKING CREEPY, CREON TELLS HER TO FUCK OFF INTO EXILE. SHE ASKS FOR ONE DAY TO GET HER SHIT SORTED OUT, AND HE SAYS SURE, NOT SEEING ANY FUCKING PLOTS OR ANYTHING THAT COULD HAPPEN HERE.

JASON THEN COMES TO SEE MEDEA AND EXPLAIN HIS SHIT. HE TELLS HER HE HAD TO DUMP HER BECAUSE SHE'S A FOREIGNER, AND WHEN HE MARRIES GLAUKE THEY CAN ALL BE ONE BIG HAPPY FUCKING FAMILY AND SHE CAN BE HIS WHORE OR SOME SHIT. SHE THEN REMINDS HIM OF THE PROMISE HE MADE TO HER IN COLCHIS THAT HE WOULD ALWAYS BE FAITHFUL TO HER, AND THINGS GET KIND OF AWKWARD.

THE KING OF ATHENS THEN RANDOMLY TURNS UP ASKING FOR FUCKING FAMILY PLANNING ADVICE. MEDEA BEGS HIM TO TAKE HER IN WHEN SHE HAS TO LEAVE CORINTH, AND HE SAYS YES. MEDEA THEN ~~STARTS~~ CONTINUES PLOTTING SHIT.

MEDEA FINDS SOME HOT-ASS CLOTHES TO GIVE TO GLAUKE AS A LOVELY WEDDING GIFT. SHE POURS POISON ALL OVER THEM, IN AN EXTREMELY MENACING WAY. SHE GETS JASON TO COME BACK AND CRIES AND LOOKS SORRY AND SHIT, AND CONVINCES HIM TO GIVE THE CLOTHES TO GLAUCE.

GLAUKE GETS SUPER FUCKING EXCITED OVER THE SHINIES, AND TRIES THEM ON IMMEDIATELY. THEN HER FUCKING SKIN STARTS BUBBLING OFF AND SHE DIES IN AGONY. FUCKING CREON TRIES TO HELP HIS DAUGHTER BY PATTING OUT THE FLAMES, BUT THE MAGIC CLOTHES STICK TO HIM AND HE FUCKING BURNS TOO. THEN HE TRIES TO ESCAPE AND ALL HIS FLESH TEARS OFF ON THE CLOTHES. PRESUMABLY MEDEA COATED THEM IN FUCKING SUPERGLUE AS WELL AS MAGIC.

THEN THERE'S THIS WEIRD ALTERNATE STORY WHERE ZEUS FALLS IN LOVE WITH MEDEA HERE (BECAUSE DOUBLE-MURDER IS SO FUCKING HOT), BUT SHE JUST SAYS FUCK NO TO HIM.

MEDEA MOVES ON TO PHASE TWO OF HER EVIL FUCKING PLAN TO GET BACK AT JASON FOR BEING SUCH A DICK. SHE FUCKING KILLS THEIR CHILDREN. WHAT A BITCH.

ALTERNATIVELY THE PEOPLE OF CORINTH KILL THE KIDDIES, AND SUPPOSEDLY THEY BRIBED EURIPIDES TO WRITE THAT BIT OUT OF HIS LOVELY PLAY SO THEY SEEM LIKE NICE GUYS. FUCKING CORINTHIANS.

THEN MEDEA FLIES OFF TO ATHENS IN A FUCKING "DRAGON WAGON". IT'S A FLYING CHARIOT. DRAWN BY MOTHERFUCKING DRAGONS. WITH THE BODIES OF HER DEAD CHILDREN ON THE BACK. THEY SEE HER ROLLING AND EVERYONE'S SERIOUSLY FUCKING HATING THE CREEPY WITCH.

AND THE MORAL OF THAT STORY IS NEVER CHEAT ON AN INSANE MURDEROUS WITCH. IT'S A FUCKING TERRIBLE IDEA.

PENTHEUS HAS PROBLEMS WITH WOMEN

ONE DAY PENTHEUS, WHO IS THE KING OF THEBES AND A COMPLETE SHITWEASEL, DECIDES TO BAN WORSHIP OF DIONYSUS.

NATURALLY, DIONYSUS ISN'T AT ALL PLEASED BY THIS. NOT ONE FUCKING BIT. HE PROVOKES ALL THE WOMEN IN THEBES INTO A BACCHIC FRENZY AND THEY TEAR ALL THEIR CLOTHES OFF AND RUN UP THE NEAREST MOUNTAIN TO DANCE.

PENTHEUS COMES HOME TO FIND HIS MUM AND HIS AUNTS MISSING, AND WHEN HE FINDS OUT THAT THEY'RE DANCING AROUND NAKED HALF WAY UP A MOUNTAIN HE'S PRETTY FUCKING ANNOYED. HE GETS HIS MEN TO CAPTURE DIONYSUS AND PUT HIM IN PRISON.

DIONYSUS IS A GOD, SO HE JUST WALKS STRAIGHT OUT OF THE PRISON, AND SITS BACK TO WATCH WHAT HAPPENS NEXT.

PENTHEUS SNEAKS OUT OF THE CITY AND GOES UP THE MOUNTAIN TO PERV ON HIS MUM AND HIS AUNTS. UNFORTUNATELY FOR HIM, THEY'RE TEMPORARILY INSANE. THAT'S WHAT A BACCHIC FRENZY DOES. THEY SPOT HIM HIDING IN A BUSH, THINK HE'S AN ANIMAL, AND TEAR HIS ARMS AND LEGS OFF. WITH THEIR FUCKING BARE HANDS.

THAT'S WHAT YOU GET FOR GETTING IN THE WAY OF DIONYSUS.

HADES DOESN'T UNDERSTAND DATING

PERSEPHONE IS THE DAUGHTER OF DEMETER, THE GODDESS OF FERTILITY.

ONE DAY, SHE'S PLAYING IN A FIELD WITH A BUNCH OF SHITTY NYMPHS, WHEN HADES (WHO IS ONE SAD LONELY MOTHERFUCKER WHO DOESN'T QUITE UNDERSTAND THINGS LIKE FLIRTING OR CONSENT) JUMPS OUT OF A HOLE IN THE GROUND, STICKS A FUCKING BAG OVER HER HEAD, AND DRAGS HER DOWN TO THE UNDERWORLD TO BE HIS WIFE. THE NYMPHS DON'T EVEN TRY TO STOP HIM. NYMPHS DON'T GIVE A SHIT ABOUT ANYONE EXCEPT THEMSELVES.

WHEN DEMETER FINDS OUT THAT HER DAUGHTER HAS BEEN FUCKING KIDNAPPED, SHE SULKS AND REFUSES TO LET ANY PLANTS GROW TILL PERSEPHONE IS RETURNED AND HADES SAYS SORRY.

IN THE END ZEUS GETS FED UP WITH THIS WINTER BULLSHIT AND SHOUTS AT HADES UNTIL HE GIVES PERSEPHONE BACK. UNFORTUNATELY, PERSEPHONE DIDN'T THINK TO REFUSE FOOD OFFERED TO HER BY THE CREEPY MOTHERFUCKER THAT FUCKING ABDUCTED HER, SO BECAUSE SHE ATE HIS FOOD SHE HAS TO GO BACK TO THE FUCKING UNDERWORLD FOR HALF OF THE YEAR EVERY SINGLE FUCKING YEAR.

WHENEVER SHE ISN'T HOME, DEMETER SULKS AGAIN, AND THAT'S HOW FUCKING WINTER HAPPENS.

MIDAS

LOOKING FOR THE BEST FUCKING CHRISTMAS/CELEBRATION OF YOUR CHOICE GIFT? BUY THEM GOLD. GOLD IS ALWAYS FUCKING GREAT.

UNLESS YOU'RE FUCKING MIDAS. MIDAS IS KING OF PHRYGIA (WHERE THE STUPID FUCKING HATS COME FROM). ONE DAY, SILENUS, ONE OF DIONYSUS' DRINKING BUDDIES, GETS COMPLETELY FUCKING TRASHED AND LOSES THE PARTY HE WAS AT (SHIT HAPPENS OK).

MIDAS SEES THIS DRUNK SATYR STUMBLING AROUND AND THINKS THAT THIS WOULD BE A PERFECT FUCKING XENIA OPPORTUNITY, SO HE LURES SILENUS TO HIS PALACE WITH SOME MORE DRINK. ALTERNATIVELY HE TIES SILENUS UP WITH FLOWERS TO FORCE HOSPITALITY UPON HIM. WHAT A FUCKING GUY.

EITHER WAY MIDAS IS SUPER FUCKING NICE TO SILENUS, SO DIONYSUS GIVES HIM A WISH IN RETURN. INSTEAD OF WISHING FOR MORE WISHES OR TO FREE THE GENIE OR SOME SHIT LIKE THAT, HE WISHES FOR ALL THAT HE TOUCHES TO TURN TO FUCKING GOLD. WHILE THIS SEEMS LIKE A GREAT IDEA FOR ABOUT FIVE FUCKING MINUTES AS HE BECOMES SUPER RICH, IT SOON GETS SUPER FUCKING SHITTY WHEN ALL HIS FOOD TURNS TO MOTHERFUCKING GOLD AND HE CAN'T EAT OR DRINK.

HE THEN BEGS DIONYSUS TO TAKE THE GIFT BACK (HE'D KEPT THE FUCKING RECEIPT AND EVERYTHING!). DIONYSUS CAN BE A PRETTY CHILL DUDE SOMETIMES (WHEN HE'S NOT TURNING PEOPLE CRAZY/INTO DOLPHINS) SO HE TELLS HIM TO JUST GO FOR A SWIM IN A LOCAL RIVER. MIDAS DOES SO, THEN EVERYTHING WAS FUCKING FINE.

HE BECOMES A FUCKING HIPPY AND FUCKS OFF TO LIVE IN THE HILLS, WHERE HE OVERHEARS PAN AND APOLLO HAVING SOME SHITTY LITTLE MUSIC CONTEST. BEING A BIT OF AN ASSHOLE AND NOT HAVING LEARNT THAT THE GODS ARE SUPER POWERFUL AND WILL FUCK SHIT UP, MIDAS BUTTS IN AND SAYS THAT PAN SHOULD WIN (ALTHOUGH EVERYONE ELSE HAS

DECIDED THAT APOLLO, GOD OF FUCKING MUSIC, IS BETTER). APOLLO THEN SAYS HE MUST HAVE THE EARS OF A FUCKING ASS (NOT BUTT-EARS. THAT WOULD BE MAYBE TOO WEIRD), SO HE GIVES MIDAS FUCKING DONKEY EARS.

MIDAS THEN RUNS FURTHER FROM CIVILISATION, COVERING HIS EARS UP WITH A FUCKING PHRYGIAN CAP.

TAKING A JOYRIDE IN YOUR DAD'S WHEELS

PHAETHON'S FRIEND IS CALLING HIS MOTHER A SLUT, AND SAYING THAT PHAETHON'S DADDY ISN'T A GOD. THIS IS CLASSICAL MYTH, OF COURSE HIS FATHER'S A GOD. PHAETHON DOUBLE CHECKS WITH HIS MOTHER, FINDING THAT HE WAS THE SON OF THE SUN. YES THE FUCKING SUN (HELIOS / SOL / PHOEBUS / GREAT BIG GLOWY THING IN THE FUCKING SKY).

PHAETHON'S SHITTY FRIEND STILL DOESN'T BELIEVE HIM, AND PHAETHON WANTS FURTHER PROOF. SO HE GOES TO TALK TO THE FUCKING SUN (WHO LIVES SOMEWHERE BEYOND INDIA, DON'T YOU FUCKERS KNOW ANYTHING?). ANYWAY, HE CHECKS WITH HIS DADDY THAT HE IS INDEED THE SON OF THE SUN. HELIOS IS SO PLEASED THAT HE'S BOTHERED TO DRAG HIS ASS ALL THE WAY TO SEE HIM THAT HE PROMISES HIM ONE WISH.

NATURALLY PHAETHON ASKS FOR THE MOST STUPID FUCKING PIECE OF SHIT WISH IMAGINABLE: TO DRIVE HIS DAD'S FLAMING CHARIOT FOR THE DAY (HELIOS TRAVELS ACROSS THE SKY IN A FLAMING CHARIOT EVERY DAY, IT'S KIND OF LIKE FUCKING SANTA AND HIS REINDEER BUT MORE FIERY). PRESUMABLY FACE-PALMING, HELIOS IS FUCKING PISSED OFF AT THIS BECAUSE IT'S STUPIDLY DANGEROUS, ALSO BECAUSE HE'S BEEN DUMB ENOUGH TO SWEAR ON THE STYX TO DO ANY FUCKING THING HIS RECKLESS LITTLE SON ASKS. HE EXPLAINS TO PHAETHON WHY THIS WAS SUCH A STUPID-ASS THING TO ASK, HOW HE'S GOING TO DIE A HORRIBLE FIERY DEATH AND HOW IT'LL BE GENERALLY CRAP, BUT PHAETHON ISN'T PUT OFF.

SO HELIOS GIVES HIS SON SOME MAGIC SUN-CREAM AND A QUICK CRASH COURSE IN SUN-CHARIOT FLYING AND SENDS HIM OFF. OF COURSE, PHAETHON MAJORLY FUCKS UP. HE GETS TO THE TOP OF THE SKY, BUT THEN LOOKS DOWN AND GETS FUCKING SCARED, SO HE DROPS THE REINS. THE HORSES FUCK AROUND AND EVENTUALLY HE ENDS UP FLYING SUPER CLOSE TO AFRICA (HOW DID YOU FUCKING THINK THE SAHARA DESERT WAS CREATED?).

THIS PISSES ZEUS OFF (A LOT OF THINGS PISS ZEUS OFF) BECAUSE THIS KID IS CLEARLY BREAKING THE FUCKING CELESTIAL

HIGHWAY CODE. INSTEAD OF TAKING POINTS OFF PHAETHON'S LICENCE, ZEUS JUST FUCKING ZAPS HIM WITH HIS LIGHTNING, AND PHAETHON FALLS DEAD OUT OF THE SKY, INTO A RIVER. HE THEN GETS TURNED INTO A CONSTELLATION, SO THIS STORY DOES HAVE A HAPPY FUCKING ENDING AFTER ALL.

ARACHNE

ARACHNE IS SOME LYDIAN BITCH WHO GETS FUCKING FAMOUS FOR BEING SUPER GOOD AT WEAVING AND SHIT. SHE'S SO FUCKING GOOD THAT SHE MAKES THE TOTAL DICK-MOVE OF SAYING SHE'S BETTER THAN FUCKING ATHENA. WHAT THE FUCK, GIRL? HAVEN'T YOU HEARD OF HUBRIS?

ATHENA ROCKS UP CUNNINGLY DISGUISED AS AN OLD LADY. ARACHNE IS HAVING NONE OF THAT OLD LADY SHIT AND STARTS OFFENDING HER, NOT KNOWING WHO THE FUCK IT IS. THIS PISSES ATHENA OFF EVEN MORE SO SHE DITCHES THE DISGUISE AND GOES BACK TO LOOKING STUNNING.

WHEN ALL THAT BITCHING IS OVER, THEY GET ON WITH THEIR SHITTY LITTLE "GREAT LYDIAN WEAVE-OFF". ATHENA MAKES THIS SWEET-ASS TAPESTRY WITH PICTURES OF THE GODS BEING BAMFS ON IT. ARACHNE MAKES ONE WITH COOL-ASS MYTHOLOGICAL SCENES (MAINLY OF THE GODS FUCKING WITH MORTALS). ARACHNE'S IS BETTER. THIS IS SERIOUSLY FUCKING AWKWARD AND ATHENA GETS HELLA MAD AND TEARS IT UP.

POOR ARACHNE IS SO UPSET ABOUT THE SHIT SHE'D GOT HERSELF INTO THAT SHE HANGS HERSELF. ATHENA IS A TOTAL BITCH AND WON'T LET HER DIE. INSTEAD SHE TURNS HER INTO A NASTY-ASS SPIDER, SO IT'S ARACHNE'S DESCENDANTS THAT ARE RIGHT NOW CREEPING OVER YOUR WALLS, DOWN FROM YOUR CEILINGS AND ONTO YOUR TERRIFIED FACES

COCKBLOCKED BY A WALL

PYRAMUS AND THISBE ARE TWO HOT TEENAGERS LIVING NEXT DOOR TO EACH OTHER SOMEWHERE IN THE EAST. BEING HOT TEENAGERS IN CLOSE PROXIMITY, THEY FALL MADLY IN LOVE, EVEN THOUGH THEIR DICKISH PARENTS WON'T EVEN LET THEM MEET.

THEIR ENTIRE FUCKING RELATIONSHIP IS BASED AROUND TALKING THROUGH A SMALL HOLE IN A WALL. THEY ARRANGE TO MEET OUT BY SOME TOMB (FUCKING ROMANTIC LOCATION RIGHT THERE).

THISBE ARRIVES EARLY, BUT THERE'S THIS FUCKING LION COVERED IN BLOOD ALREADY TAKING ADVANTAGE OF THE ROMANTIC SPOT. THISBE FUCKS OFF LIKE ANY SANE FUCKER WOULD, DROPPING HER STUPID HEAD-PIECE. EVENTUALLY PYRAMUS TURNS UP AND FREAKS THE FUCK OUT BECAUSE HE ASSUMES THIS LION HAS EATEN THISBE (BUT WHAT IF THISBE WAS THE FUCKING LION? THEY'VE NEVER ACTUALLY FUCKING MET, REMEMBER).

PYRAMUS SUDDENLY KILLS HIMSELF BECAUSE HE'S A LOVESTRUCK TEENAGER IN A MYTH AND THERE'S NOT MUCH ELSE HE CAN DO. THISBE EVENTUALLY SHOWS UP AND IS FUCKING PISSED THAT LOVER BOY HAS BEEN SUCH AN IDIOT, SO SHE KILLS HERSELF TOO.

NOBODY KNOWS WHAT THE FUCK HAPPENED TO THE LION, BUT ON THE UPSHOT THE GODS TURNED MULBERRIES RED IN HONOUR OF THEIR LOVE OR SOME SHIT LIKE THAT.

IT'S BASICALLY ROMEO AND FUCKING JULIET BUT WITH A COCKBLOCKING LION.

PYGMALION

PYGMALION IS A GREAT BIG BAG OF DICKS WHO THINKS EVERY WOMAN AROUND IS A COMPLETE WHORE AND NOT GOOD ENOUGH FOR A FUCKER LIKE HIM. UNSURPRISINGLY, HE'S SERIOUSLY FUCKING SINGLE. WHEN HE ISN'T BEING A DICK ABOUT WOMEN, HE'S SCULPTING SHIT.

ONE DAY PYGMALION CARVES A HOT-ASS STATUE OF A SEXY LADY. THIS SHIT-WEASEL LOVES HOW HIS STATUE CAN'T EXPRESS OPINIONS, RUN AWAY FROM HIM IN DISGUST OR BE A SLUT. HIS PERFECT FUCKING WOMAN. HE FALLS COMPLETELY IN LOVE WITH HER AND BRINGS HER SHITTY LITTLE STONES AS PRESENTS AND THEN STARTS TO DO SEXY THINGS WITH THE STATUE [SIDE NOTE: REAL-LIFE PRAXITELES' APHRODITE OF KNIDOS SUPPOSEDLY HAD CUM STAINS ON HER BUTT FROM PEOPLE TRYING TO FUCK THE FUCKING STATUE].

EVENTUALLY PYGMALION PLUCKS UP THE COURAGE TO AWKWARDLY ASK THE GODS TO GIVE HIM A GIRL AS AWESOME AS HIS STATUE. APHRODITE FEELS SORRY FOR THIS FEDORA-WEARING LOSER, AND AS HE AND HIS STATUE ARE MAKING OUT, APHRODITE TURNS HER INTO A REAL GIRL. THEY ENDUP WITH KIDS AND A FUCKED UP MARRIAGE DYNAMIC. PYMALION'S A DICK BASICALLY.

PAN FUCKS EVERYTHING

ALL THE GREEK GODS SLEEP AROUND ONE HELL OF A LOT. HERMES ONCE GOT A GIRL PREGNANT WITH A HALF GOD, HALF GOAT MONSTER GOD THING, LATER KNOWN AS PAN. PAN HAD A PRETTY FUCKED UP LIFE. WHEN HIS MOTHER LOOKED AT HER NEW BABY, HE WAS SO FUCKING HIDEOUS THAT SHE SCREAMED AND RAN AWAY. AS A RESULT, PAN ISN'T VERY GOOD WITH WOMEN.

PAN IS THE GOD OF NATURE, SO HE SPENDS MOST OF HIS TIME SLEEPING AND PLAYING WITH SHEEP AND BEES. AND NYMPHS. LOTS OF NYMPHS. PAN FUCKED ALL THE NYMPHS. LITERALLY. HE COLLECTED THEM.

ONCE HE TRIED TO RAPE A NYMPH CALLED PITYS, WHO TURNED INTO A TREE, BECAUSE THAT'S WHAT NYMPHS DO WHEN THEY GET SCARED. IT'S LIKE HEDGEHOGS ROLLING UP INTO BALLS, OR POSSUMS PRETENDING TO BE DEAD, ONLY IT'S KIND OF PERMANENT, WHICH DEFEATS THE FUCKING POINT.

THEN HE TRIED TO RAPE SYRINX, WHO.... YES, THAT'S RIGHT. TURNED INTO A FUCKING PLANT. SHE RAN AWAY TO THE RIVER AND TURNED INTO A REED, AT WHICH POINT PAN GOT CONFUSED AND HADN'T A FUCKING CLUE WHICH REEDS WERE REEDS AND WHICH WERE NYMPHS, SO HE CUT THEM ALL DOWN AND MADE PIPES OUT OF THEM. CREEPY BASTARD.

AT ONE POINT HE COVERED HIMSELF IN WOOL AND PRETENDED TO BE A SHEEP TO SEDUCE SELENE. PRESUMABLY HE WAS A REALLY FUCKING SEXY SHEEP. EITHER THAT OR SELENE HAD SOME FUCKED UP KINKS.

GANYMEDE

GANYMEDE IS A HOT DUDE (WELL, KID REALLY) FROM FUCKING TROY. HE'S SUPER PRETTY AND MAKES THE MISTAKE OF STEPPING OUTSIDE TO HERD SOME SHEEP OR SOME SHIT. ZEUS SPOTS HIM.

ZEUS CLEARLY REALISES THE RAPING AND LEAVING TECHNIQUE ISN'T FUCKING WORKING FOR HIM, SO HE TURNS INTO A FUCKING EAGLE TO KIDNAP GANYMEDE AND TAKE HIM BACK TO HIS FUCKING LOVE NEST.

ZEUS KINDA LIKES THIS GANYMEDE FUCKER, SO HE MAKES HIM IMMORTAL SO HE CAN BE THE FUCKER WHO SERVED HIS DRINKS. THIS IS ALSO TO PISS HERA OFF, AS THERE'S NOTHING SHE HATES MORE THAN OTHER PEOPLE WHO ZEUS HAS FUCKED.

BUT DON'T YOU FUCKERS GO THINKING THIS KIDNAP IS AT ALL FUCKING UNFAIR. ZEUS GIVES GANYMEDE'S DAD SOME RIDICULOUSLY FUCKING BADASS HORSES AS COMPENSATION, WHAT A FUCKING NICE GUY.

GANYMEDE GETS A PLACE IN A FUCKING CONSTELLATION TOO AND KINDA BECOMES THE GOD OF GAY LOVE.

OWLBEARS?

POLYPHONTE LIKES TO FROLIC. SHE LIKES TO FROLIC SO FUCKING MUCH THAT SHE TELLS APHRODITE TO FUCK OFF AND SPENDS HER LIFE FUCKING AROUND WITH ARTEMIS.

APHRODITE IS A VINDICTIVE BITCH, THOUGH, SO SHE DRIVES POLYPHONTE MAD AND GETS HER TO FALL IN LOVE WITH A MOTHERFUCKING ANGRY BEAR. POLYPHONTE IS REALLY FUCKING DETERMINED, SO SHE SOMEHOW MANAGES TO FUCK THE BEAR. ARTEMIS FREAKS THE FUCK OUT, BECAUSE THIS SHIT IS FUCKED UP, AND SETS ALL THE ANIMALS IN THE WOODS ON HER. POLYPHONTE PANICS AND RUNS HOME TO HER DAD'S HOUSE, WHERE SHE GIVES BIRTH TO TWO FUCKING MASSIVE HAIRY CANNIBAL BABIES.

ZEUS IS FUCKING HORRIFIED, SO HE SENDS HERMES DOWN TO PUNISH POLYPHONTE AND THE CANNIBAL BEAR BABIES BY CUTTING OFF THEIR FUCKING HANDS AND FEET. FORTUNATELY FOR THEM, ARES RESCUES THEM. LESS FORTUNATELY, ARES IS FUCKING SHIT AT RESCUING, SO INSTEAD OF PROPERLY SAVING THEM HE JUST TURNS THEM INTO FUCKING OWLS. HOOT HOOT MOTHERFUCKERS.

ACTAEON

ACTAEON IS THIS YOUNG DUDE WHO IS FOR ONCE NOT A COMPLETE ASSHOLE, HE'S JUST SERIOUSLY FUCKING UNLUCKY. ONE DAY HE'S ON A HUNT, AND EVERYTHING IS FUCKING GREAT. THEN HE WANDERS OFF INTO A CLEARING WHERE ARTEMIS IS HAVING A BATH. BIG FUCKING MISTAKE

HER NYMPHS ALL RUN TO COVER HER UP, BUT ACTAEON HAS ALREADY SEEN HER LADY THINGS SO SHE'S CRAZY PISSED OFF ABOUT THIS. SHE DOESN'T WANT ANY MORTAL FUCKERS TALKING ABOUT HER BEING NAKED, SO SHE JUST TURNS ACTAEON INTO A FUCKING STAG. THIS IS ALWAYS A GOOD SOLUTION TO ALL YOUR PROBLEMS.

ACTAEON FUCKS OFF, BUT TO BEGIN WITH DOESN'T REALISE HE'S A DEER. HE EVEN GETS HAPPY TO HEAR THE REST OF THE HUNTING PARTY COMING TO FIND HIM. EXCEPT HE'S NOW A DEER. AND BITCHES HUNT DEER.

ACTAEON GETS RIPPED TO PIECES BY HIS OWN DOGS, AND OVID EVEN FUCKING NAMES ALL OF HIS DOGS (HE HAS A SHIT TONNE) (ALSO ONE IS CALLED 'SPOT').

EOS FUCKS GENDER ROLES

HAVE YOU HAD IT WITH ALL THESE MOTHERFUCKING GODS SEDUCING MOTHERFUCKING MORTAL WOMEN? THEN YOU'LL LOVE EOS, GODDESS OF FUCKING DAWN, WHO'S RATHER INTO STEALING MEN.

ONE TIME EOS SLEPT WITH ARES. THIS PISSED OFF HIS GIRLFRIEND APHRODITE, SO SHE CURSED EOS WITH BEING HORNY ALL THE FUCKING TIME. BONUS POINTS FOR CREATIVITY.

SO EOS STARTS KIDNAPPING AND SEDUCING MORTAL MEN, SO NOW NOBODY IS SAFE. ~~NOBODY WAS EVER SAFE FROM ZEUS' GOD-WANG.~~

EOS' MOST FAMOUS STOCKHOLM SYNDROME VICTIM IS TITHONUS, WHO BECOMES HER OFFICIAL BLOKE. HE'S SOME TROJAN FUCKER (PRIAM'S BROTHER) AND SUPER HOT, SO EOS GETS HER ROSY FINGERS ALL OVER HIM.

SHE WANTS TITHONUS TO BE IMMORTAL, SO SHE GOES AND BEGS ZEUS FOR IT. ZEUS IS COOL WITH THAT, SO TITHONUS LIVES FOREVER. BUT EOS IS SO DISTRACTED BY THAT BOOTY THAT SHE FORGETS TO ASK FOR TITHONUS TO BE FOREVER YOUNG AND CUTE (MAYBE SHE'S NOT VERY BRIGHT, FOR DAWN).

TITHONUS JUST GETS SUPER FUCKING OLD AND EVENTUALLY TURNS INTO A GRASSHOPPER FOR NO CLEAR REASON, BUT THAT'S OF COURSE WHY GRASSHOPPERS ARE NOISY AT DAWN: BECAUSE THEY'RE EXCITED ABOUT SEEING EOS. CUTE.

CANNIBAL DINNER-PARTIES SUCK

LYCAON IS A KING OF ARCADIA, GREECE, AND A BIT OF A DICK.

THIS IS BACK IN THE DAYS WHEN THE GODS WOULD JUST RANDOMLY SHOW UP FOR DINNER AT MORTALS' HOUSES. ONE DAY ZEUS ROCKS UP AT LYCAON'S PLACE AND SAYS "I'M ZEUS GET ME SOME FUCKING CHICKEN".

LYCAON, BEING THE DICK HE IS, THINKS THIS WOULD BE A FUN TIME TO SEE IF THE GODS ARE REALLY THAT FUCKING GREAT. SO HE THROWS A DINNER PARTY FOR ZEUS, AND COOKS UP SOME MAN-FLESH (POSSIBLY HIS OWN FUCKING SON) INTO SOME KIND OF "MYSTERY MEAT SURPRISE".

LYCAON ALSO PLANS TO TRY AND STAB ZEUS A BIT LATER IF HE FALLS ASLEEP. WHAT THE FUCK, DUDE, THAT AIN'T XENIA. ANYWAY, WHEN THE MEAL IS SERVED ZEUS KNOWS WHAT FUCKERY HAS GONE DOWN. SO HE FLIPS THE TABLE AND DESTROYS THE ENTIRE FUCKING HOUSE WITH LIGHTNING.

FINALLY HE TURNS LYCAON INTO A FUCKING WOLF SO HE HAS TO SPEND THE REST OF HIS LIFE DOING ASSHOLE WOLF THINGS.

HE ALSO KILLS ALL FIFTY OF LYCAON'S SONS FOR GOOD MEASURE, BECAUSE ZAPPING FUCKERS WITH LIGHTNING IS FUCKING AWESOME.

CALLISTO

CALLISTO, DAUGHTER OF LYCAON, IS ONE OF ARTEMIS' ~~BACKING DANCERS~~ HUNTING GANG, SWORN TO BE A VIRGIN AND ALL THAT SHIT. ONE DAY SHE GOES SOLO AND WANDERS OFF ON HER OWN. THIS IS GENERALLY NOT A GREAT FUCKING IDEA IN MYTHICAL GREECE, MOTHERFUCKERS.

UNFORTUNATELY, ZEUS SEES HER WANDERING OFF AND FOLLOWS. HIS CREATIVE DISGUISE THIS TIME IS ARTEMIS, HIS OWN FUCKING DAUGHTER. HE IMPERSONATES HER AND SIDLES UP TO CALLISTO. MAYBE SHE AND ARTEMIS ARE A THING, WHO FUCKING KNOWS. EITHER WAY SHE DOESN'T SEEM TOO SURPRISED AT A COUPLE OF KISSES. SOON SHE REALISES THIS IS NOT ARTEMIS BUT IT'S ZEUS AND WHAT THE FUCK CAN YOU DO. ONE THING LEADS TO ANOTHER AND SHE GETS PREGNANT WITH HIS SON.

SOME TIME LATER CALLISTO, (REAL) ARTEMIS AND THE NYMPH GANG ARE SPLASHING AROUND IN A RIVER, AND IT'S KIND OF FUCKING OBVIOUS THAT CALLISTO IS PREGNANT. ARTEMIS GETS SUPER FUCKING MAD AND TELLS CALLISTO TO FUCK RIGHT OFF BECAUSE SHE'S BROKEN THE ~~BROWNIE~~ PROMISE. SHE HAS TO GO AND GIVE BIRTH ALL ALONE IN THE MOUNTAINS (KINDA SUCKS CONSIDERING HER FORMER BEST FRIEND WAS A GODDESS OF FUCKING CHILD-BIRTH), AND THEN GIVES HER SON AWAY IN SHAME.

HERA OF COURSE FUCKING HATES CALLISTO, BECAUSE ZEUS LIKED HER. SO SHE TURNS CALLISTO INTO A GREAT BIG FUCKING MAMA BEAR, BECAUSE WHY THE FUCK NOT. GIVEN THAT CALLISTO'S DAD WAS TURNED INTO FREAKY WOLF-MAN, FAMILY RE-UNIONS MUST HAVE BEEN FUCKING GREAT.

CALLISTO'S SON GROWS UP AND SOME TIME LATER HE GOES HUNTING. OF COURSE HE SEES HIS MOTHER, BUT DOESN'T RECOGNISE HER BECAUSE HE'S NOT A FUCKING GENIUS. HE'S ABOUT TO THROW A SPEAR AT HER, BUT IN THE NICK OF TIME ZEUS TURNS MOTHER AND SON INTO THE CONSTELLATIONS URSA MAJOR AND MINOR. FUCKING STARS, MAN. IS THIS A HAPPY ENDING? WHO THE FUCK KNOWS.

ZEUS AND HERA

BEFORE HE MARRIES HERA, ZEUS HAS ALREADY HAD A FLING WITH HIS SISTER, DEMETER. MAMA RHEA IS THEREFORE PRETTY FUCKING WORRIED ABOUT ZEUS GETTING WITH HIS OTHER SISTERS.

WHATEVER THE REASON, ZEUS GOES TO SOME FUCKING COVERT EFFORT TO SEDUCE HERA; HE TURNS INTO A FUCKING CUCKOO AND SHOWS UP (SADLY NOT FROM A CLOCK) AND HERA TAKES HIM IN AS A PET.

THIS IS ALL GOING WELL UNTIL SURPRISE MOTHERFUCKER IT'S YOUR HORNY BROTHER. HERA IS PRESUMABLY SOMEWHAT SURPRISED, BUT SEEMINGLY SHE JUST FUCKING ROLLS WITH IT, AS SOON THEY HAVE A WEDDING PLANNED.

THIS IS A DAMN BIG WEDDING; ALL OF THE GODS AND NYMPHS AND SERIOUSLY FUCKING ANYONE OF IMPORTANCE GET AN INVITATION. THE ONLY ONE NOT TO SHOW UP IS SOME DUMB NYMPH WHO'S TOO BUSY BITCHING ABOUT HOW STUPID THIS WEDDING IS. SO HERMES SHOWS UP, CHUCKS HER HOUSE INTO A RIVER AND TURNS HER INTO A MOTHERFUCKING TORTOISE.

AS WELL AS YOUR USUAL KITCHEN-APPLIANCE BASED WEDDING GIFTS, GAIA GIVES HERA SOME BITCHIN' APPLE TREES AND A BADASS DRAGON TO GUARD THEM AGAINST ASSHOLES LIKE HERACLES.

OH AND A COUPLE OF VERSIONS SAY THEIR WEDDING NIGHT LASTS FOR 300 YEARS. DAAAAAMN.

AGDISTIS

DURING ONE OF HIS FUCKED-UP SEXY ADVENTURES, ZEUS ACCIDENTALLY GETS THE EARTH PREGNANT. THE BABY IS AGDISTIS, WHO IS A HERMAPHRODITE WITH MOTHERFUCKING SUPERPOWERS. THE GODS ARE SO FUCKING DISTURBED THAT THEY CASTRATE AGDISTIS, AND AS SOON AS THE TESTICLES LAND THEY TURN INTO FUCKING ALMOND TREES.

AGDISTIS GOES ON TO HAVE A WIDE RANGE OF SEXY ADVENTURES, CULMINATING IN GETTING FUCKING ENGAGED TO THE DAUGHTER OF KING ATTES. UNFORTUNATELY, WHEN AGDISTIS GETS NAKED AFTER THE FUCKING WEDDING CEREMONY, ATTES GOES COMPLETELY FUCKING INSANE, CUTS HIS OWN DICK OFF, AND BLEEDS TO DEATH.

AGDISTIS IS REALLY FUCKING SORRY, MAGICS THE BODY SO IT'LL NEVER DECOMPOSE, AND GOES TO LIVE A SAD LIFE ALONE IN THE WOODS. IT'S FUCKING TRAGIC.

IXION IS A COMPLETE SHIT-BUCKET

IXION IS ENGAGED TO DIA, BECAUSE HE PROMISED HER DADDY A SHIT TONNE OF GIFTS. UNFORTUNATELY FOR HER FATHER, IXION'S A COMPLETE ASSHOLE AND ISN'T GOING TO GIVE ANY FUCKER A GIFT. INSTEAD, HE SETS A FUCKING BOOBY TRAP FOR HIS FATHER-IN-LAW AT THE WEDDING FEAST.

THIS AIN'T SOME SHITTY PRACTICAL JOKE, IXION FUCKING BURNS HER FATHER ALIVE.

WHILST EVERYONE THINKS THIS IS PRETTY DICKISH BEHAVIOUR, ZEUS THINKS IT'S FINE BECAUSE HE'S DONE CRAZIER SHIT WHEN IN LOVE, AND HE INVITES IXION OVER FOR DINNER.

BUT IXION IS AN UNGRATEFUL DICK, SO HE DECIDES TO RAPE HERA WHILE HE HAS THE CHANCE. ZEUS IS THE KING OF THE FUCKING GODS, OF COURSE HE KNOWS WHAT FUCKERY IXION HAS PLANNED. HIS SOLUTION? HE MAKES A FAKE HERA OUT OF CLOUDS.

IXION IS COMPLETELY SHIT-FACED SO HE DOESN'T REALISE HE'S FUCKING A CLOUD-CLONE. IT HAPPENS. SURPRISE SURPRISE, ZEUS WALKS IN ON THEM AND HAS IXION STRAPPED TO A SPINNING FIRE WHEEL OF DEATH FOREVER.

CLOUD-CLONE LADY HAS A SON BY IXION, CENTAURUS. CENTAURUS GETS FREAKY WITH SOME HORSES AND THAT, FRIENDS, IS WHERE CENTAURS COME FROM.

WINE OR POISON?

ICARUS (NO NOT THAT ICARUS) IS FRIENDS WITH A BUNCH OF SHEPHERDS, AND THEY ALL SPEND THEIR TIME DICKING AROUND IN THE SUN POINTLESSLY. ONE DAY, DIONYSUS COMES TO VISIT ICARUS AND GIVES HIM A BOTTLE OF WINE. UP TO THIS POINT, NOBODY HAS A FUCKING CLUE WHAT WINE IS. THEY'VE NEVER SEEN IT BEFORE.

ICARUS SHARES HIS BOTTLE OF WINE WITH HIS FUCKING SHEPHERD FRIENDS, AND THEY ALL GET COMPLETELY FUCKING WASTED. ICARUS LEAVES FOR A MINUTE TO GO FOR A SHIT, AND AT THAT POINT ONE OF HIS OTHER FRIENDS COMES OVER TO FIND A BUNCH OF FUCKING SHEPHERDS LYING ON THE FLOOR LOOKING REALLY FUCKING CONFUSED AND OCCASIONALLY THROWING UP. ASSUMING THAT ICARUS HAS FUCKING POISONED ALL THE SHEPHERDS, HE GETS AN ANGRY MOB TOGETHER AND WAITS FOR ICARUS TO COME BACK. AS SOON AS ICARUS COMES HOME, THE ANGRY MOB MURDER THE SHIT OUT OF HIM, CUT HIM INTO FUCKING TINY PIECES, AND THROW THE PIECES INTO THE MOTHERFUCKING WELL.

SOME TIME LATER, ICARUS' DOG MAERA COMES TO VISIT HIS DAUGHTER ERIGONE AND BARKS AT HER. IN TRUE LASSIE-STYLE, ERIGONE WORKS OUT THAT MAERA WANTS TO TELL HER THAT ICARUS HAS FALLEN DOWN THE WELL. SHE DOESN'T WORK OUT THAT HE'S BEEN MANGLED INTO TINY FUCKING PIECES THOUGH, SO WHEN SHE GETS TO THE WELL SHE GETS A PRETTY FUCKING HUGE SURPRISE.

TRAUMATISED BY THE SIGHT OF HER DAD LYING AT THE BOTTOM OF THE WELL IN A HEAP OF BLOODY FUCKING MEAT LUMPS, ERIGONE HANGS HERSELF FROM THE NEAREST TREE. THEN MAERA THE DOG HURLS HERSELF DOWN THE WELL IN A DESPERATE BID FOR SUICIDE AND BREAKS HER NECK. NOW EVERYONE'S DEAD AND IT'S A FUCKING TRAGEDY.

MAGIC SNAKEY KISSES

THE TREE OUTSIDE MELAMPUS' HOUSE HAS A MOTHERFUCKING SNAKE INFESTATION. WHAT A WONDERFUL PROBLEM TO HAVE. THE SNAKEBUSTERS COME AND KILL MOST OF THE BIG SNAKES, BUT LEAVE THE SAD LITTLE ORPHAN SNAKELETS.

MELAMPUS IS SUCH A NICE FUCKING GUY THAT HE ADOPTS THE BABY SNAKELETS AND LOOKS AFTER THEM. IN RETURN, THE SNAKES LICK HIS EARS WHILE HE SLEEPS. IT'S HOW SNAKES SHOW LOVE, OK.

WHEN HE WAKES UP MELAMPUS CAN BASICALLY TALK TO ANIMALS AND SEE THE FUTURE, BECAUSE THESE ARE HELLA MAGIC SNAKELETS AND THEY LOVE HIM SO FUCKING MUCH.

ONE TIME MELAMPUS GETS KIDNAPPED, BUT LISTENS TO THE WOODWORMS IN THE HOUSE TELLING HIM IT'S ABOUT TO FALL DOWN. HE TELLS HIS KIDNAPPERS THIS AND SURPRISINGLY THEY LET HIM GO BECAUSE THEY'RE SOME REALLY NICE KIDNAPPERS.

THE HOUSE FALLS DOWN AND MELAMPUS RUNS AWAY TO BE PROPHET. MORAL OF THE STORY: ADOPT ALLLLLLLL THE SNAKELETS.

BLIND DATE

DAPHNIS IS YOUR AVERAGE ABANDONED-AT-BIRTH-RAISED-IN-THE-FIELDS DEMI-GOD. THEY'RE COMMON AS FUCK OK. ANYWAYS, HE'S SUPER INTO FUCKING WITH COWS (NOT LITERALLY, YOU DIRTY MOTHERFUCKER) AND SINGING AND HUNTING WITH ARTEMIS AND ALL THAT JAZZ.

ONE DAY HE FALLS IN LOVE WITH A SUPER HOT NYMPH. DOESN'T EVERYONE? HE'S A CUTE LIL FUCKER AND PROMISES NEVER TO SLEEP WITH ANYONE ELSE. SHE DOESN'T QUITE TRUST HIM AND SAYS SHE'LL FUCK HIM UP IF HE CHEATS.

THIS LASTS ALL OF FIVE MINUTES, BECAUSE DAPHNIS GETS DRUNK AND ENDS UP FUCKING SOME PRINCESS. OOPS. HIS NYMPH GIRLFRIEND FINDS OUT AND IS UNDERSTANDABLY PRETTY FUCKING PISSED OFF. SO SHE SMASHES HIS MOTHERFUCKING EYES OUT. ALTERNATIVELY SHE TURNS HIM INTO A ROCK. THAT'S SOME STONE COLD REVENGE SHIT RIGHT THERE.

DAPHNIS WANDERS AROUND THE COUNTRYSIDE SINGING SADLY BECAUSE HE'S SOME REAL PRETENTIOUS LOSER. HE GETS SO INTO HIS MUSIC THAT HE WANDERS OFF A MOTHERFUCKING CLIFF AND SPLATTERS HIMSELF TO DEATH. WHAT A FUCKING DISASTER OF A PERSON.

LEANDER FORGETS HIS WATER-WINGS

THE HERO OF OUR STORY, LEANDER, LIVES ON ONE SIDE OF THE HELLESPONT. OUR HEROINE, HERO (FUCK OFF), IS A PRIESTESS OF APHRODITE LIVING IN A (TOTALLY NOT PHALLIC) TOWER ON THE OTHER SIDE OF THE HELLESPONT. THEY END UP MEETING AT SOME RAD-ASS FESTIVAL, AND THERE'S LOVE AT FIRST SIGHT AND ALL THAT CRAP.

INITIALLY HERO DOESN'T WANT TO FUCK LEANDER, BECAUSE SHE'S SUPPOSED TO BE SUPER CHASTE AND PRIESTESSY. BUT THEN HE MAKES THE FUCKING GREAT POINT THAT SHE'S THE PRIESTESS OF THE MOTHERFUCKING SEX GODDESS, AND APHRODITE IS ALWAYS PRO-SEXY-TIMES.

UNFORTUNATELY, HERO'S FOLKS ARE SUPER PROTECTIVE OF HER, AND LEANDER ALSO LIVES FORTY MILES OF SEA AWAY FROM HER. BUT NOTHING WILL STOP THIS FUCKER GETTING SOME, SO EVERY NIGHT HE FUCKING SWIMS THE HELLESPONT TO FUCK HER. DAMN, THAT'S COMMITMENT, BUT HAS THIS FUCKER NOT HEARD OF A BOAT?

THEY HAVE A HAPPY SUMMER OF SEXY TIMES, THEN AUTUMN COMES AND THE SEA GETS HELLA NASTY. BUT LEANDER IS SUCH A HORNY MOTHERFUCKER THAT HE IGNORES THE CURRENT AND THE WINDS AND ALL THAT SHIT, AND SWIMS OUT. HE FUCKS UP AND DROWNS, BECAUSE HE SHOULD HAVE LISTENED TO THE FUCKING SHIPPING FORECAST. HIS BODY WASHES UP OUTSIDE HERO'S TOWER AND SHE GETS REALLY FUCKING UPSET AND JUMPS INTO THE SEA TO JOIN HIM. HA HA LIKE YOU WERE EXPECTING A HAPPILY EVER AFTER.

ECHO DON'T NEED NO MAN

YOU FUCKERS ALL KNOW THE CUTE STORY ABOUT ECHO AND THAT SHITDICK NARCISSUS THAT OVID USES? WELL HERE'S A DIFFERENT ONE, THIS TIME WITH MORE MESS TO GET OUT OF THE CARPET.

ECHO IS AN ADORABLE HIPPIE NATURE-FUCKING NYMPH LADY. EXCEPT SHE AIN'T FUCKING NO NATURE BECAUSE SHE'S PURER THAN THOU. ONE DAY PAN (HALF MAN, HALF GOAT, ALL PASTORAL RAPE GOD) SEES HER AND WANTS TO TAP THAT.

SHE TELLS HIM TO FUCK RIGHT OFF BECAUSE SHE'S HAVING FUN SINGING AND ENJOYING NATURE AND ALL THAT FUCKERY. HER SINGING IS A MAJOR TURN-ON FOR PAN, AND ALSO HE'S REALLY FUCKING JEALOUS OF HOW TALENTED SHE IS.

BEING LIKE 90% (A) DICK, PAN THEN MAKES ALL THE LOCAL SHEPHERD TYPES GO BATSHIT CRAZY AND FUCKING *RIP ECHO APART*. WHO THE FUCK DOES THAT? SHE STILL WON'T STOP SINGING THOUGH, BECAUSE YOU CAN'T STOP THE BEAT AND ALL THAT SHIT.

SO WHEN YOU FUCKERS HEAR AN ECHO SOMEWHERE, THAT'S JUST A TINY PIECE OF SOME NICE LADY WHO GOT FUCKING SCATTERED ACROSS THE COUNTRYSIDE.

KING MINOS' SON GETS IN A STICKY SITUATION

AFTER ALL THAT FUCKERY WITH HIS BULL MONSTER STEP-SON, MINOS COMPLETELY FORGETS ABOUT HIS LITTLE SON GLAUKOS. ONE DAY GLAUKOS IS PLAYING IN THE PALACE AND FALLS IN A MASSIVE POT OF HONEY AND DROWNS BECAUSE HE'S A STUPID FUCK. WHO THE FUCK JUST LEAVES A BIG THING OF HONEY LYING AROUND? THIS IS NOT A CHILD-SAFE ENVIRONMENT YOU STUPID MOTHERFUCKER.

A WHILE LATER, MINOS NOTICES HIS SON IS MISSING. HE ROUNDS UP A BUNCH OF SEERS TO FIND THE KID, AND EVENTUALLY SOME FUCKER POLYEIDOS (WHO IT TURNS OUT IS ALSO VERY GOOD AT DESCRIBING COWS OR SOME SHIT LIKE THAT) FINDS THE VERY STICKY AND VERY DEAD BOY. MMM. HONEY.

MINOS FREAKS THE FUCK OUT BECAUSE HE CAN'T BRING HIS SON BACK TO LIFE AND HE'S AN IRRATIONAL FUCKER. HE THEN LOCKS POLYEIDOS IN PRISON WITH THE STICKY STICKY CORPSE UNTIL HE RESURRECTS HIM. MINOS IS AN EXCELLENT PROBLEM SOLVER OK.

EVENTUALLY A SNAKE RANDOMLY APPEARS IN THE CELL AND POLYEIDOS MURDERS IT TO DEATH BECAUSE HE'S A DICK. A SECOND SNAKE SHOWS UP AND IS SAD ABOUT ITS DEAD FRIEND, SO IT FEEDS IT A MAGIC PLANT AND SOON THE SNAKE IS ALIVE AGAIN. WE DON'T REMEMBER THIS SHIT BEING IN BIO CLASS. ANYWAY, POLYEIDOS WATCHES THIS SHIT AND FINDS SOME MORE OF THE MAGIC PLANT, AND THEN FEEDS IT TO THE DEAD KID.

SUDDENLY GLAUKOS IS ALIVE AND EVERYONE IS HAPPY. EXCEPT POLYEIDOS WHO'S NOT ALLOWED TO LEAVE CRETE UNTIL HE TEACHES THIS MAGIC SHIT TO GLAUKOS. BUT THEN THE STICKY FUCKER SPITS INTO POLYEIDOS' MOUTH AND FORGETS IT? TOTALLY HOW MEMORY WORKS YES.

ORION

ONE DAY ZEUS, HERMES AND POSEIDON ARE HAVING AN ADVENTURE. THEY STOP AT SOME FUCKER HYRIEUS' PLACE AND HE'S SO FUCKING NICE THEY GRANT HIM ONE FAVOUR.

HYRIEUS WANTS A SON, SO THE BOYS GET BUSY. THEY GET A COW'S SKIN, THEN THEY ALL PISS ON IT. YES. THEY BURY IT, AND NINE MONTHS LATER A SUPER ATTRACTIVE GIANT IS BORN, AND GETS NAMED ORION.

ORION'S FIRST WIFE IS A FUCKING IDIOT AND MANAGES TO GET THROWN INTO TARTARUS BY HERA FOR BEING AN ARROGANT FUCK. NEXT ORION GOES AFTER SOME GIRLCALLED MEROPE.

HE GOES AROUND KILLING ALL OF THE WILD BEASTS ON HER HOME ISLAND OF CHIOS (ORION FUCKING LOVES HUNTING SHIT), BUT HER DADDY STILL THINKS THIS MASSIVE GIANT ISN'T A GOOD GUY FOR HIS DAUGHTER. SO ORION RAPES HER. WHAT A FUCKING ASSHOLE. HER DAD GETS HIM BACK BY STABBING HIS FUCKING EYES OUT AND TELLING HIM TO FUCK RIGHT OFF.

ORION INDEED FUCKS OFF AND THROUGH SOME BULLSHIT INVOLVING THE SUN GETS HIS FUCKING SIGHT BACK. HE THEN GOES OFF TO BE ARTEMIS' HUNTING BFF, AND THEY PISS AROUND IN THE WILDERNESS FOR A BIT.

ONE VERSION SAYS ARTEMIS KILLS HIM WHEN SHE REALISES WHAT A DOUCHBAG HE IS WHEN HE ATTEMPTS TO RAPE ONE OF HER GIRL-GROUP.

ALTERNATIVELY HE BOASTS THAT HE CAN KILL ALL THE FUCKING BEASTS IN THE ENTIRE FUCKING WORLD, SO GAIA (MAMA EARTH) SENDS A BOSS-ASS SCORPION TO KILL THE FUCK OUT OF HIM. THEN THEY BOTH BECOME STARS, BECAUSE WHAT ELSE WOULD STARS BE MADE FROM?

ROMAN MYTHOLOGY

THE AENEID: BOOK I

JUNO SERIOUSLY FUCKING HATES ALL THE TROJANS. UNFORTUNATELY FOR OUR HERO AENEAS, HE'S A FUCKING TROJAN. AENEAS IS SAILING OFF TO FOLLOW HIS DESTINY AND SHIT, BUT JUNO WON'T STAND FOR THAT KIND OF CRAP, SO SHE CONVINCES THE WINDY GUY AEOLUS (BY PROMISING TO GET HIM LAID) TO MAKE A HUGE STORM TO FUCK SHIT UP FOR AENEAS. GOOD GUY NEPTUNE CALMS THE STORM BEFORE ANYONE IMPORTANT DIES OR ANYTHING, SO ALL IS GOOD.

AENEAS AND FRIENDS EVENTUALLY END UP ON A BEACH IN NORTH-AFRICA, AND HAVE A HUGE FUCKING BARBECUE. MEANWHILE BACK AT OLYMPUS, VENUS (AENEAS' MILF) RUNS OFF TO HER DADDY JUPITER, CRYING ABOUT HOW EVERYTHING IS SHITTY FOR HER SON AND HOW JUNO IS BEING A BITCH. JUPITER TELLS HER TO CALM THE FUCK DOWN AND THAT AENEAS IS GOING TO GO ON TO FATHER A LINE OF FUCKERS WHO EVENTUALLY FOUND ROME WHICH IS GOING TO HAVE THE GREATEST FUCKING EMPIRE BLAH BLAH ROME IS FUCKING AWESOME BLAH BLAH BLAH.

VENUS THEN GOES DOWN TO VISIT AENEAS, DRESSED SOMEWHAT INAPPROPRIATELY FOR VISITING HER SON AS A SEXY HUNTING LADY. SHE GIVES HIM SOME FUCKING USEFUL TOURIST INFORMATION ABOUT THE LAND HE'S IN THEN FUCKS OFF. BASICALLY AENEAS IS A COMPLETE MUMMY'S BOY AND THERE'S NOTHING THAT WILL PERSUADE US OTHERWISE.

AENEAS GOES TO CARTHAGE (WHICH IS KIND OF A CONSTRUCTION SITE RIGHT NOW SO ALL THESE TROJANS JUST GET IN THE WAY), HE CRIES AT SOME PAINTINGS FOR A BIT (HE'S SENSITIVE, FUCK OFF) THEN MEETS DIDO. DIDO IS A CRAZY STALKER LADY WHO KNOWS EVERYTHING ABOUT AENEAS BEFORE SHE'S EVEN MET HIM. THIS IS FUCKING CREEPY.

THEN VENUS DECIDES TO MAKE THINGS MORE FUN BY HAVING DIDO FALL COMPLETELY IN LOVE WITH AENEAS. SHE DOES THIS BY GETTING CUPID TO TURN INTO A CREEPY-ASS CLONE OF AENEAS' YOUNG SON ASCANIUS. CREEPY BABY-CLONE CUPID

SITS ON DIDO'S LAP IN A COMPLETELY NON-WEIRD WAY AND POISONS HER WITH LOVE. THIS WILL RUIN DIDO'S FUCKING LIFE.

AENEAS AND THE TROJANS PARTY HARD WITH THE CARTHAGINIANS, UNTIL DIDO ASKS FOR STORY TIME ABOUT WHAT THE FUCK HAPPENED AT TROY.

THE AENEID: BOOK II

INTENSE TROY FLASHBACK, MOTHERFUCKERS

BACK AT TROY, THE GREEKS ARE COMPLETELY DONE WITH NOT GETTING TO FUCK SHIT UP BECAUSE THE TROJANS ARE HIDING BEHIND THEIR WALLS. SO THEY PLOT. THAT'S WHAT GREEKS FUCKING DO. THE GREEKS MAKE A HUGE FUCKING WOODEN HORSE IN A COMPLETELY NON-SUSPICIOUS WAY, THEN FUCK OFF IN THEIR SHIPS IN A NON-SUSPICIOUS WAY. THE LYING DOUCHEBAG GREEK DUDE SINON TELLS THE TROJANS THAT THE ASSHOLE GREEKS HAVE FUCKED OFF FOR GOOD, AND THE SUPER-SUSPICIOUS WOODEN HORSE THAT'S FAINTLY MAKING PEOPLE NOISES IS IN FACT A GIFT FOR MINERVA.

THE TROJANS COMPLETELY FUCKING BUY THIS (EXCEPT FOR LAOCOON, WHO HAS HAD IT WITH THESE MOTHERFUCKING GREEKS WITH THEIR MOTHERFUCKING GIFTS, SO NATURALLY HE GETS SAVAGELY KILLED BY SOME HUGE FUCKING SNAKES). THE TROJANS DRAG THE SUSPICIOUS HORSE INTO THE CITY, THEN GET COMPLETELY FUCKING WASTED AND PASS OUT. ALL IS GREAT, EXCEPT FUCKING CASSANDRA WHO'S COMPLAINING ABOUT DOOM OR SOME SHIT BUT NOBODY CARES ABOUT HER.

AENEAS MEANWHILE IS HAVING SOME TRIPPY DREAM. HE SEES HECTOR (THE SHINY FUCKER - LESS SHINY NOW HE'S A MANGLED GHOST). HECTOR TELLS AENEAS ABOUT HIS DESTINY AND SHIT AND TO GET THE FUCK OUT OF TROY. AENEAS RUNS OUTSIDE TO SEE EVERYTHING ON FUCKING FIRE BECAUSE THE GREEKS HAVE SHOWN UP TO FUCK EVERYTHING UP, BUT ALL OF THE TROJANS ARE EITHER DEAD OR SERIOUSLY HUNGOVER. AENEAS STUPIDLY JUMPS INTO HERO MODE AND RUNS OUT TO FIGHT AND ENDS UP WATCHING (AND DOING FUCKING

NOTHING) AS PYRRHUS (ACHILLES' SUPER ASSHOLE SON) HACKS OLD DUDE PRIAM TO PIECES WITH AN AXE.

AENEAS GETS THE FUCK AWAY FROM THE CRAZY AXE-MURDERER BUT RUNS INTO HELEN AND GOES TO KILL HER. MUMMY VENUS STEPS IN BECAUSE SHE FUCKING LIKES HELEN, AND ALSO BECAUSE AENEAS IS BEING A LITTLE SHIT AND IGNORING HIS DESTINY. VENUS GIVES AENEAS GOD-VISION SO HE CAN SEE HOW TRULY FUCKED TROY IS, AND AENEAS FINALLY DECIDES TO LEAVE. HE GOES BACK TO PICK UP HIS OLD DADDY ANCHISES, BUT ANCHISES CLINGS TO HIS HOME AND IS HAVING NONE OF AENEAS' SHIT.

LIKE THE SHITTIEST MOST DYSFUNCTIONAL FAMILY HOLIDAY, AENEAS WON'T LEAVE WITHOUT DADDY, SO FUCKS OFF AGAIN TO FIGHT. HIS WIFE CREUSA STOPS HIM BY WAVING THEIR BABY ASCANIUS IN HIS FACE. THE BABY PROMPTLY CATCHES ON FIRE. THAT'S WHAT BABIES FUCKING DO. ANCHISES GETS REALLY FUCKING EXCITED ABOUT THIS AND WAVES AT JUPITER TO GIVE ANOTHER OMEN. THIS TIME IT'S A SUPER OBVIOUS COMET POINTING TOWARDS ITALY.

FINALLY AENEAS PICKS DADDY ANCHISES UP ON HIS BACK, HOLDS HANDS WITH ASCANIUS (AND KEEPS CREUSA BEHIND HIM, WHERE SHE BELONGS). THEN THEY FUCK OUT OF TROY. CONVENIENTLY FOR THE PLOT, CREUSA WANDERS OFF AND IS LEFT BEHIND. GOOD FUCKING GOING AENEAS. BUT EVERYTHING IS MADE OK WHEN HE BUMPS INTO HER GHOST AND SHE TELLS HIM TO FUCK OFF AND GET ON WITH HIS DESTINY.

THE AENEID: BOOK III

EPIC FLASHBACKS CONTINUE

AFTER TROY, AENEAS SAILS AROUND MANY SHITTY PLACES IN THE MEDITERRANEAN. KINDA LIKE FUCKING ODYSSEUS, BUT AENEAS' TRIP HAS BLEEDING TREES, ORACLES, RANDOM PLAGUES, HARPIES AND HOMOEROTIC WRESTLING. BASICALLY, MORE FUN.

EVENTUALLY AENEAS GETS BORED OF THAT SHIT SO THE TROJANS WIND UP IN EPIRUS (MODERN ALBANIA). AENEAS IS SERIOUSLY FUCKING LUCKY BECAUSE ANDROMACHE, HECTOR'S WIDOW, LIVES THERE. ANDROMACHE HAS MARRIED HELENUS (ANOTHER OF PRIAM'S SONS), AND TELLS AENEAS WHAT A SHITTY TIME SHE HAD MARRIED TO PYRRHUS, BUT PYRRHUS WAS KILLED BY ORESTES (WASN'T EVERYONE?) SO NOW EVERYTHING IS FUCKING GREAT.

HELENUS AND ANDROMACHE SHOW AENEAS THEIR SHITTY LITTLE VERSION OF TROY THEY'VE BUILT, BUT AENEAS ISN'T SOLD BECAUSE DESTINY AND SHIT. HELENUS TELLS AENEAS THAT EVERYTHING IS GOING TO BE SHIT FROM NOW ON, BUT AFTER THINGS WILL WORK OUT (AS IF ALL THE CRAP THAT HAS HAPPENED SO FAR DIDN'T MAKE THAT OBVIOUS).

AENEAS AND HIS GANG THEN LEAVE QUICKLY BEFORE ANDROMACHE KIDNAPS ASCANIUS (SHE GOES CRAZY MATERNAL ON THE POOR KID). THEN THEY RESUME COPYING THAT ASSBAG ODYSSEUS' STYLE BY SAILING OVER TO THE CYCLOPS ISLAND (THEY EVEN MEET SOME ASSHOLE THAT ODYSSEUS LEFT BEHIND THERE), AND MAKE THE RATIONAL CHOICE OF SAILING THE FUCK OUT OF THAT SHIT. AENEAS THEN HAS THE SCYLLA/CHARIBDIS CHOICE THAT ODYSSEUS HAD, BUT INSTEAD JUST FUCKING AVOIDS THE ENTIRE THING. BASICALLY AENEAS IS BETTER THAN ODYSSEUS. FUCK YOU GREEKS, ROMAN PRIDE 5EVA!

THEN OLD ANCHISES SUDDENLY DIES. IN TWO FUCKING LINES. FUCK YOU VIRGIL.

THE AENEID: BOOK IV

BACK IN REAL TIME, HEARING AENEAS' ADVENTURES MAKES DIDO SO CRAZY IN LOVE WITH AENEAS THAT SHE BECOMES A PILLOW-SNIFFING FREAK, THEN (EVEN CREEPIER) SHE STARTS CLINGING ON TO ASCANIUS BECAUSE HE LOOKS LIKE A TINY AENEAS. CREEPY MOTHERFUCKER.

MEANWHILE JUNO IS MOMENTARILY PISSED THAT DIDO IS CRAY-CRAY AND SAD (JUNO FUCKING LOVES CARTHAGE AND ITS PEOPLE). SHE AND VENUS THEN PLAN A WEDDING. VENUS GOES ALONG WITH ALL THIS SHIT, LETTING JUNO THINK SHE'S TRICKED HER, BUT REALLY SHE KNOWS THAT JUPITER IS GOING TO SAY FUCK NO TO ALL OF THESE SILLY ALLIANCES.

SO DIDO AND AENEAS GO HUNTING, THERE'S A CONVENIENT STORM AND THEY END UP HAVING STEAMY CAVE SEX. DIDO CALLS IT A FUCKING MARRIAGE, NO BITCH, YOU DON'T GET TO MARRY AENEAS. DIDO'S NEIGHBOUR IARBAS IS FUCKING JEALOUS ABOUT THIS BECAUSE HE WANTED TO FUCK THE QUEEN, SO HE BITCHES TO HIS DADDY (CONVENIENTLY, JUPITER).

JUPITER FINALLY INTERVENES WITH THIS SHIT AND GETS MERCURY TO TELL AENEAS TO GET THE FUCK OUT OF CARTHAGE AND GET ON WITH HIS DESTINY BULLSHIT. DIDO FINDS OUT ABOUT THIS AND GOES BATSHIT, THEN AENEAS IS A COMPLETE DOUCHEBAG AND GIVES HER THE WORST FUCKING BREAK-UP SPEECH EVER. DIDO TRIES BEING ANGRY, BUT FAINTS DRAMATICALLY.

AENEAS AND GANG PLAN TO SNEAK AWAY WITHOUT DIDO KNOWING, BUT SHE FINDS OUT ANYWAY AND THEN JUST GETS CRAZIER AND BECOMES OBSESSED WITH WEIRD CULTS. AENEAS EVENTUALLY FUCKS OFF, AND AS HE DOES DIDO BUILDS A HUGE FUCKING FIRE AND BURNS HIS STUFF HE LEFT BEHIND. SHE THEN STABS HERSELF AND JUMPS IN THE FIRE TOO. BUT AENEAS ISN'T ALLOWED TO GIVE TWO FUCKS BECAUSE DESTINY AND SHIT.

THE AENEID: BOOK V

AENEAS SAILS OFF FROM CARTHAGE, NOTICING A MASSIVE FUCKING FUNERAL PYRE. A SINGLE MANLY FUCK TRICKLES DOWN HIS CHEEK TRAGICALLY. SOON HE FORGETS DIDO AND FUCKS OFF TO SICILY.

SICILY IS WHERE OLD DADDY ANCHISES DIED A YEAR AGO. OF COURSE, WHEN FUCKERS DIE IN THE ANCIENT WORLD, IT'S TIME FOR A FUCKING PARTY! FIRST THERE'S A BOAT RACE, WHICH INVOLVES AN OLD DUDE BEING THROWN IN THE FUCKING SEA (EVERYONE LAUGHS AS HE STRUGGLES TO SWIM, ASSHOLES). EVERYONE WINS A SHIT TONNE OF PRIZES.

THEN THERE'S A RUNNING RACE THAT INVOLVES PEOPLE FALLING IN COW SHIT AND CHEATING AND BASICALLY TROJANS ARE ASSHOLES. EVERYONE WINS A SHIT TONNE OF PRIZES. NEXT THERE'S A BOXING MATCH WHERE SOME OLD FUCKER GOES CRAZY AND ALMOST KILLS SOME YOUNG DUDE. EVERYONE WINS A SHIT TONNE OF PRIZES. FINALLY THERE'S ARCHERY AND IT ALL GOES CRAZY WHEN SOMEONE'S ARROW FUCKING CATCHES ON FIRE. EVERYONE WINS A SHIT TONNE OF PRIZES.

WHILST THE MEN ARE HAVING A GREAT FUCKING TIME, THE WOMEN ARE BEING WHINY AND ARE COMPLETELY FUCKING DONE WITH THIS SAILING SHIT. THIS IS ALL BECAUSE FUCKING JUNO HAS SENT IRIS TO GO AND MAKE ALL THE WOMEN APESHIT. THE WOMEN GO FUCKING MENTAL AND BURN SOME OF THE SHIPS. EVENTUALLY AENEAS TELLS MOST OF THE WOMEN AND OTHER LAZY ASSHOLES TO JUST FUCK OFF AND BUILD THEIR OWN SHITTY CITY IN SICILY.

ANCHISES' GHOST THEN RANDOMLY APPEARS FOR AENEAS AND TELLS HIM HE HAS SOME SUPER IMPORTANT SHIT TO TELL HIM, BUT HE CAN'T POSSIBLY TELL HIM RIGHT NOW BECAUSE HE NEEDS ALL OF BOOK SIX FOR THAT SHIT.

VENUS THEN WHINES TO NEPTUNE ABOUT AENEAS HAVING A SHITTY TIME, AND HE PROMISES TO BE NICE TO AENEAS AND LET HIM SAIL. AENEAS FUCKS OFF IN HIS BOAT, AND DOESN'T EVEN FUCKING NOTICE WHEN HIS HELMSMAN GETS TIRED AND FALLS OFF THE FUCKING BOAT.

THE AENEID: BOOK VI

AENEAS FUCKS OFF TO VISIT THE SIBYL (CRAZY OLD PROPHET LADY). WHEN AENEAS SHOWS UP SHE GOES EVEN MORE CRAZY-SHIT AND STARTS FOAMING AND TELLS AENEAS ABOUT SOME PROPHECY SHIT INVOLVING A WAR IN ITALY. MASSIVE FUCKING SURPRISE RIGHT THERE.

AENEAS IS A WHINY SHIT AND WANTS TO VISIT THE FUCKING UNDERWORLD LIKE EVERY OTHER FUCKING BIG NAME HERO HAS. HE GETS SOME SHITTY GOLDEN TWIG FOR PROSERPINA (QUEEN BITCH DOWNSTAIRS), THEN THE SIBYL (WHO IS LESS CRAZY NOW) LEADS HIM DOWN THROUGH THE CREEPY ASS CAVERNS FULL OF SHIT TONNES OF MONSTERS.

THE UNDERWORLD IS GENERALLY REALLY CRAPPY, FULL OF UNHAPPY DEAD PEOPLE WAILING AND MOANING AND SHIT. THERE'S ALSO AN ENTIRE AREA OF JUST DEAD BABIES. FUCKING STRANGE. AENEAS SEES DIDO'S GHOST IN THE PEOPLE-WHO-DIED-FOR-LOVE ZONE, BUT DIDO JUST FUCKING BLANKS THE LITTLE SHIT AND FUCKS OFF WITH HER ACTUAL HUSBAND.

AENEAS TALKS TO A SHIT TONNE OF DEAD PEOPLE AND IT'S BASICALLY JUST LIKE THE SUPER ROMAN VERSION OF ODYSSEY BOOK XI. AT LAST AENEAS BUMPS INTO DEAD DADDY ANCHISES AND HE GETS SUPER FUCKING EXCITED BECAUSE HE FINALLY GETS TO SHOW AENEAS THE "PARADE OF FUTURE ROMANS" WHICH WOULD BE A SHIT TONNE MORE FUN IF IT WERE LIKE A FUCKING DISNEY PARADE OR SOMETHING. BASICALLY ALL OF THE ROMANS ARE GOING TO BE FUCKING AWESOME, ESPECIALLY THAT AUGUSTUS FUCKER, HE'S THE FUCKING BEST.

THE BOOK ENDS WITH AENEAS LEAVING THROUGH THE "GATE OF IVORY" WHICH IS BASICALLY THE GATE OF LIES SO EFFECTIVELY THIS WHOLE FUCKING BOOK WAS ONE BIG LIE, ASSHATS.

THE AENEID: BOOK VII

AENEAS IS PISSING AROUND IN ITALY EATING SOME CRAPPY FRUIT.

MEANWHILE, THE SHIT IS GOING DOWN IN LATIUM (AN AREA OF ITALY). THERE'S FUCKING BEES ALL OVER THIS SPECIAL FUCKING TREE. FUCK OFF BEES. ALSO, THE KING OF LATIUM'S DAUGHTER, LAVINIA, RANDOMLY CATCHES ON FIRE. WHAT THE FUCK LAVINIA. LATINUS, THE KING OF THE LATINS IN FUCKING LATIUM (SERIOUSLY THINK OF SOME BETTER FUCKING NAMES VIRGIL) INTERPRETED THESE FUCKED UP EVENTS AS GOOD OMENS. FUCK YES.

AENEAS SENDS SOME OF HIS ~~HOMIES~~ ROMIES TO TALK TO LATINUS ABOUT BASICALLY STEALING HIS FUCKING KINGDOM. SURPRISINGLY, LATINUS IS COMPLETELY FUCKING DOWN FOR THIS, AND GIVES EVERYONE A FUCKING PONY (A SOMEWHAT INSENSITIVE GIFT FOR A TROJAN). HE EVEN PROMISES THAT AENEAS CAN MARRY LAVINIA (DESPITE HER ALREADY BEING ENGAGED, AWKWARD).

EVERYTHING IS WAY TOO HAPPY FOR JUNO. SO SHE SENDS MOTHERFUCKING ALLECTO (A FUCKING FURY) TO FUCK SHIT UP. ALLECTO THROWS HER FUCKED UP SNAKE HAIR THINGS AT AMATA, THE QUEEN OF LATIUM, MAKING HER GO BATSHIT CRAZY AND TRY TO STOP THE MARRIAGE BETWEEN AENEAS AND LAVINIA. THEN AMATA JUST FUCKS OFF INTO THE WOODS IN A CRAZY MANNER, SPREADING HER CRAZY.

NEXT ALLECTO GOES TO TURNUS, PRINCE OF THE RUTULIANS, LAVINIA'S NOW EX-FIANCE AND A BIT OF A SHIT. IT DOESN'T TAKE MUCH (JUST A BURNING TORCH) TO MAKE HIM GO FUCKING CRAZY AND WANT WAR. FINALLY SHE GOES TO ASCANIUS AND MAKES HIM GO JUST A LITTLE BIT CRAZY SO HE KILLS THIS SPECIAL FUCKING PET STAG.

KILLING BAMBI'S DAD MAKES THE COUNTRY BUMPKINS NEARBY GO CRAZY SHIT AND START FIGHTING THE TROJANS. WAR HAS FUCKING STARTED, BITCHES. JUNO LAUGHS EVILLY, EVERYTHING IS GOING ACCORDING TO PLAN. THE BOOK ENDS

WITH A LONG LIST OF ALL THE FUCKERS WHO ARE HERE TO FIGHT. IT'S VERY ILIAD II. ALSO TURNUS HAS A BEAUTIFUL FUCKING HELMET.

THE AENEID: BOOK VIII

THE GOD OF THE FUCKING RIVER TIBER SHOWS UP IN AENEAS' DREAMS AND TELLS HIM TO GET HIS SHIT TOGETHER (ALSO TO BE NICE TO JUNO BECAUSE SHE'S PPRETTY FUCKING PISSED OFF). SO AENEAS GOES TO VISIT "ROME" TO LOOK FOR SOME HELP. BUT IT'S NOT ROME YET, IT'S JUST SOME SHITTY VILLAGE WITH CATTLE FUCKING EVERYWHERE AND SOME SHITTY PIGLETS, RULED BY OLD DUDE EVANDER.

AENEAS MEETS EVANDER AND THEY IMMEDIATELY BECOME BEST FRIENDS BECAUSE THEY'RE VERY VERY DISTANTLY RELATED, ALSO EVANDER IS A MASSIVE TROY FAN-BOY. THEN EVANDER GIVES AENEAS A TOUR OF NOT-ROME AND TELLS HIM STORIES ABOUT THE TIME HERCULES CAME THERE AND BEAT UP SOME CATTLE THIEF.

MEANWHILE VENUS IS WORRIED ABOUT HER POOR LITTLE BABY BOY, SO SHE PERSUADES HER HUSBAND VULCAN TO MAKE AENEAS SOME PRETTY ARMOUR. VULCAN GETS TO FUCKING WORK.

EVANDER THEN RANDOMLY TELLS AENEAS ABOUT SOME COMPLETE DICKWAD MEZENTIUS WHO WAS SUCH A SHITTY LEADER HE GOT KICKED OUT OF HIS CITY AND BUDDIED UP WITH TURNUS. AENEAS GETS HELLA EXCITED ABOUT FIGHTING, BECAUSE THAT'S BASICALLY ALL HE'S GOOD AT. EVANDER SENDS HIS SON PALLAS OUT TO FIGHT WITH AENEAS.

THE BOOK ENDS WITH A SUPER DETAILED DESCRIPTION OF AENEAS' PRETTY NEW SHIELD. IT'S COVERED IN PICTURES OF ROMANS LIKE AUGUSTUS BEING BADASS MOTHERFUCKERS.

THE AENEID: BOOK IX

JUNO TELLS TURNUS TO GET HIS SHIT TOGETHER AND ATTACK THE TROJANS' CRAPPY LITTLE CAMP WHILE AENEAS IS OFF PLAYING WITH PALLAS. TURNUS TRIES TO BURN THE TROJANS' SHIPS FIRST, BUT THEY FUCKING TURN INTO SEA-NYMPHS AND ESCAPE. FUCKING PLOT TWIST.

TURNUS WAS EXPECTING THE TROJANS TO COME OUT AND FIGHT HIM, BUT THEY'RE ALL "FUCK NO. FUCK OFF TURNUS" AND STAY BEHIND THEIR WALLS.

NISUS AND EURYALUS, SUPER ADORABLE TROJAN BOYFRIENDS, THINK IT WILL BE A GREAT IDEA TO SNEAK PAST ALL OF THE FUCKING RUTULIANS SURROUNDING THE CAMP AND TELL AENEAS ALL THE SHIT GOING DOWN BACK AT THE RANCH.

THEY CREEP OUT IN THE MIDDLE OF THE NIGHT BUT ARE SOON GIVEN AWAY BY EURYALUS' SPARKLY HELMET. FUCKING KILLER FASHION CHOICES HERE. THEY RUN AWAY BUT EURYALUS IS WEARING SO MUCH FUCKING BLING THAT HE CAN'T KEEP UP. EVENTUALLY EURYALUS IS KILLED, AND SO IS NISUS, BUT ONLY AFTER HE STABS THE FUCK OUT OF EURYALUS' KILLER AND LIES DOWN NEXT TO HIS BOYFRIEND'S CORPSE TO DIE. CUTE.

THE RUTULIANS SHOW UP AGAIN AT THE TROJAN CAMP (THIS TIME WITH NISUS AND EURYALUS' HEADS ON STICKS) AND FINALLY THERE'S A PROPER FIGHT. SUDDENLY AGED-UP ASCANIUS KILLS SOME FUCKER WHO CALLED THE TROJANS A BUNCH OF GIRLS, BUT THEN APOLLO PULLS HIM OUT OF THE FIGHTING BECAUSE NOBODY WANTS LIL ASCANIUS TO DIE.

FINALLY TURNUS BREAKS INTO THE TROJAN CAMP, BUT GETS SO FUCKING CAUGHT UP IN THE FIGHTING THAT HE FORGETS ABOUT OPENING THE GATES TO LET HIS MEN IN. YOU HAD ONE FUCKING JOB TURNUS. BUT WHEN SHIT STARTS GETTING BAD FOR HIM HE JUMPS INTO THE FUCKING RIVER AND SWIMS TO FREEDOM.

THE AENEID: BOOK X

AENEAS HAS MADE MORE FRIENDS. ALL OF HIS FRIENDS HAVE BOATS AND THERE'S A HUGE FUCKING LIST. AS HE SAILS BACK TO GET SHIT DONE, AENEAS RUNS INTO THE SEA-NYMPHS THAT USED TO BE HIS OTHER BOATS. HELLA WEIRD. TURNUS AND THE RUTULIANS MEET AENEAS' BROS AT THE SHORE AND THERE'S A HUGE FUCKING BATTLE, WITH ALL THE GRAPHIC DEATHS YOU FUCKERS LOVINGLY REMEMBER FROM THE ILIAD.

AENEAS AND PALLAS KILL A SHIT TONNE OF TURNUS' GANG. EVENTUALLY PALLAS RUNS INTO TURNUS, AND HE MAKES SUCH A HEROIC FUCKING SPEECH THAT IT MAKES HERCULES CRY MANLY TEARS, BECAUSE HE KNOWS BRAVE LIL PALLAS DOESN'T STAND A CHANCE. THERE'S AN AWKWARD "MY SPEAR IS BETTER THAN YOUR SHITTY SPEAR" MOMENT, THEN TURNUS KILLS PALLAS AND TAKES HIS SHINY-ASS BELT.

AENEAS HEARS ABOUT THIS AND GOES INTO CRAZY FUCKING PSYCHO-KILLER MODE. THIS PISSES JUNO OFF BECAUSE SHE HATES THE IDEA OF AENEAS SUCCEEDING AT ANYTHING, SO SHE FUCKING BITCHES TO JUPITER ABOUT IT NOT BEING FAIR FOR POOR LIL TURNUS AND THAT VENUS IS CHEATING AND MAKING THE TROJANS TOO FUCKING GOOD. JUPITER CANNOT BE ASSED WITH JUNO'S BITCHING ANY MORE, SO HE LETS HER DO HER SHIT.

JUNO MAKES A FUCKING FAKE AENEAS TO LURE TURNUS ONTO A SHIP, THEN CUTS THE ROPES AND TURNUS AWKWARDLY SAILS THE FUCK OFF. THEN IT WAS MEZENTIUS' (TURNUS' ASSHOLE FRIEND) TIME TO SHINE. HE ENDS UP BEING ATTACKED BY AENEAS, BUT HIS YOUNG SON LAUSUS JUMPS TO HIS RESCUE. IF YOU THOUGHT AENEAS WAS A NICE MERCIFUL FUCKER THEN YOU'RE FUCKING WRONG, BECAUSE AENEAS KILLS THAT KID THEN KILLS MEZENTIUS.

THE AENEID: BOOK XI

THERE'S TONNES OF FUCKING FUNERALS FOR ALL THE DEAD FUCKERS FROM BOOK TEN. AENEAS TAKES PALLAS' BODY BACK TO HIS FATHER EVANDER AND IT'S FUCKING AWKWARD.

MEANWHILE THE LATINS ARE WONDERING WHY THE FUCK THEY ARE STILL FIGHTING, BECAUSE TURNUS IS A BIT OF A DICK WHEREAS AENEAS SEEMS LIKE A PRETTY CHILL DUDE. THIS OLD DUDE DRANCES BITCHES ABOUT TURNUS FOR A BIT. TURNUS BITCHES BACK AND AGREES THAT MAYBE SETTLING THIS SHIT WITH A DUEL WOULD BE A GREAT FUCKING IDEA.

TURNUS IS A SNEAKY BASTARD SO CLEARLY HE WAS LYING ABOUT THE DUEL, BECAUSE HE THEN PLOTS AN AMBUSH WITH BADASS LADY WARRIOR QUEEN CAMILLA.

THERE'S A MASSIVE LIST OF FUCKERS CAMILLA KILLS (SHE'S ONE OF DIANA'S FAVOURITES SO SHE'S A SERIOUS BADASS MOTHER-FUCKER). BUT SHE'S A WOMAN, AND POWERFUL WOMEN ARE FUCKING SCARY SO SHE'S QUICKLY KILLED OFF, AND WHEN SHE DOES HER ARMY FUCKS THE FUCK OFF OUT OF THERE.

TURNUS' PLOT IS FUCKED AND HE HAS NO FRIENDS LEFT. THE MOTHERFUCKING END IS NIGH.

THE AENEID: BOOK XII

LATINUS IS FUCKING PISSED AT TURNUS, BECAUSE TURNUS IS GENERALLY A DICK. EVENTUALLY EVERYONE AGREES TO HAVE SOME SHITTY DUEL TO END THIS CRAP.

THIS ANGERS JUNO. EVERYTHING FUCKING ANGERS JUNO, PEACE FOR AENEAS ESPECIALLY. JUNO CONVINCES TURNUS' SISTER JUTURNA, CONVENIENTLY A MINOR GODDESS, TO GO AND FUCK SHIT UP WITH THIS TRUCE.

AENEAS AND TURNUS RIDE OUT TO MEET EACH OTHER AND EVERYHING GOES ACCORDING TO PLAN. BUT THEN JUTURNA STARTS BITCHING ABOUT AENEAS, AND SUDDENLY THERE'S FUROR EVERY-FUCKING-WHERE.

SOME IDIOT THROWS A SPEAR AND THE TRUCE IS FUCKED. THEN SOME FUCKER HITS AENEAS WITH AN ARROW, AND HE HAS TO RETREAT. VENUS HEALS AENEAS STRAIGHT AWAY, BECAUSE SHE DOESN'T WANT HER ICKLE BABY TO HAVE AN OUCHIE. FUCKING OVER PROTECTIVE PARENTING.

MEANWHILE JUTURNA HAS CHARIOT-JACKED TURNUS AND IS DOING SOME MAD DRIVING SKILLS AROUND THE BATTLEFIELD TO PROTECT HER BROTHER. AENEAS IS GETTING BORED OF THIS SHIT SO RANDOMLY DECIDES TO ATTACK LATINUS' CITY. CALM THE FUCK DOWN AENEAS.

FINALLY TURNUS GETS HIS SHIT TOGETHER AND GOES TO FIGHT AENEAS. JUPITER FINALLY CONVINCES JUNO TO GIVE UP ON HER TROJAN HATING, AS LONG AS AENEAS' PEOPLE ALL SPEAK LATIN (CONVENIENT) JUTURNA ALSO GIVES UP WITH HER SHITTY BROTHER.

AENEAS AND TURNUS FINALLY DUEL. TURNUS IS QUICKLY WOUNDED AND BEGS FOR MERCY. AENEAS IS ABOUT TO FUCKING SAY YES, UNTIL HE SEES TURNUS' SHINY BELT, THE ONE HE'D TAKEN FROM AENEAS' BFF PALLAS. AWKWARD. AENEAS GOES FUCKING CRAZY AND STABS THE SHIT OUT OF TURNUS. FUCK YOU AND YOUR CLEMENTIA!

CERES SETS A BABY ON FIRE

AFTER THE KIDNAP INCIDENT, CERES SETS OUT TO RESCUE HER WAYWARD DAUGHTER. FOR SOME WEIRD-ASS REASON SHE DRESSES UP LIKE A REALLY FUCKING OLD LADY AND STARTS HER ROADTRIP. ON THE WAY TO PERSEPHONE, SHE RUNS INTO AN OLD MAN AND HIS DAUGHTER WHO THINK SHE LOOKS LIKE AN ADORABLE OLD GRANDMA IN NEED OF DINNER AND HUGS. THERE YOU GO, MOTHERFUCKERS: IF YOU WANT FREE STUFF ON THE ROAD, DRESS UP LIKE YOUR GRANDMA.

THE OLD MAN AND HIS DAUGHTER DRAG CERES INTO THEIR HOUSE, GIVE HER DINNER, AND START TO BE SAD ABOUT THE BABY. HE'S REALLY FUCKING ILL, AND HIS MOTHER IS STUCK UPSTAIRS DESPERATELY TRYING TO KEEP THE LITTLE SHIT ALIVE.

CERES AGREES TO HAVE A LOOK AT THE KID BECAUSE SHE'S SAD ABOUT LOSING HER OWN SPAWN, SO SHE GOES UPSTAIRS FOR A BIT OF BABY-KISSING. AS SOON AS SHE TOUCHES THE BABY, THOUGH, HE MAGICALLY BECOMES HEALTHY. THE FAMILY DON'T SUSPECT ANYTHING, THOUGH, BECAUSE THEY'RE UNBELIEVABLY FUCKING UNOBSERVANT.

IN THE MIDDLE OF THE NIGHT, CERES GETS UP OFF THE SOFA AND KIDNAPS THE BABY. SHE SNEAKS DOWNSTAIRS REALLY FUCKING QUIETLY WITH BABY TRIPTOLEMUS AND PUTS HIM IN THE FIREPLACE. THEN SHE PILES COALS UP ON HIM AND SETS THE LITTLE FUCKER ON FIRE.

HIS MOTHER HEARS THE SCREAMS OF BURNING BABY AND RUNS DOWNSTAIRS TO FIND NICE HARMLESS OLD GRANDMA COOKING HER BABY SON, GRABS HIM BY THE ANKLE AND STICKS HIM IN A BUCKET OF WATER.

CERES HAD BEEN GOING TO TRY TO MAKE THE KID IMMORTAL, BUT HIS MOTHER FUCKED IT ALL UP. POSSIBLY STEALING THE BABY AND SETTING HIM ON FIRE WAS A BIT OF A FUCKING STUPID WAY TO DO IT, AT LEAST WITHOUT WARNING THE PARENTS. ANYWAY, CERES TELLS THEM ALL TO STOP BEING SO

FUCKING STUPID, BURSTS OUT OF THE HOUSE, CLIMBS ON HER DRAGON AND FUCKS OFF INTO THE DISTANCE.

FOX BONFIRE

A KID LIVES ON A FARM SOMEWHERE NEAR ROME, AND A BUNCH OF CHICKENS KEEP GOING MISSING. IT'S THE MOTHERFUCKING FOXES. THEY KEEP GRABBING CHICKENS AND FUCKING OFF TO EAT THEM.

EVENTUALLY, THE KID FINDS ONE OF THE FOXES AND CATCHES IT IN A BAG. THEN HE SETS FIRE TO THE FUCKER. NOW THERE'S BURNING FOX EVERYWHERE. IT WAS A BIT OF A SHIT IDEA, BUT NOW IT'S TOO LATE. THE FOX RUNS AWAY SCREAMING STRAIGHT THROUGH THE CORNFIELDS AND SETS FIRE TO EVERYTHING.

NOW EVERYTHING IS ON FUCKING FIRE AND IT'S ALL THE KID'S FAULT. HE BLAMES THE FOX, THOUGH, SO IN ORDER TO PUNISH FOXES FOR BURNING THE CROPS A NEW ANNUAL TRADITION IS STARTED.

EVERY FUCKING YEAR, IN HONOUR OF CERES, A SHITLOAD OF FOXES ARE CAUGHT IN ROME, HERDED TO THE CIRCUS MAXIMUS, AND SET ON FUCKING FIRE. AND IT'S NOT EVEN THEIR FAULT. WHAT A FUCKING DISASTER.

ENGLISH AND WELSH MYTHOLOGY

A SHITTY KNIGHT

SIR CYNON IS A MOTHERFUCKING MYTHOLOGICAL WELSH KNIGHT. ALL KNIGHTS FUCKING DO IS FIGHT SHIT, SO HE GOES ON A QUEST FOR SOMETHING TO BEAT UP.

SOON HE FINDS A WEIRD FUCKER WHO LIVED IN A CASTLE WITH A SHIT TONNE OF MAIDENS. FUCKING CREEP. ANYWAY, THIS CREEP SUGGESTS GOING INTO SOME NASTY FOREST BECAUSE THERE WOULD BE SHIT THERE TO ABUSE.

SIR CYNON RIDES OUT TO THE FOREST AND FINDS SOME OGRE FUCKER WITH ONE FOOT AND ONE EYE. THIS DUDE TELLS HIM TO GO POUR SOME WATER FROM SOME SUPER SPECIAL FOUNTAIN.

HE DOES THIS AND BAM, THERE'S A MASSIVE FUCKING HAILSTORM THAT KILLS ALL THE FLUFFY BUNNIES AND ANY OTHER FUCKERS IN THE AREA, EXCEPT SIR CYNON BECAUSE HE'S A FUCKING KNIGHT.

ANOTHER KNIGHT APPEARS. WOAH THERE. THIS IS THE FUCKING BLACK KNIGHT AND HE'S A BIG SCARY ASSHOLE. SIR CYNON ACCUSES HIM OF BEING A DICKWAD FOR CAUSING THE SHITTY WEATHER.

THEN THE BLACK KNIGHT BEATS THE CRAP OUT OF SIR CYNON BECAUSE HE'S A PRETTY FUCKING CRAP KNIGHT. BEING A KNIGHT FUCKING SUCKS OK.

YOU CAN'T JUST FUCKING KILL BABY MERLIN

SOME FUCKER CALLED VORTIGERN IS TRYING TO BUILD A SHITTY CASTLE. BUT THERE'S A MASSIVE FUCKING PROBLEM - THE CASTLE KEEPS SINKING INTO THE GROUND.

THIS IS FUCKING ANNOYING, SO THE WISE OLD FUCKS SAY IT CAN ONLY BE FIXED BY SPRINKLING A CHILD'S BLOOD ALL OVER THE PLACE. BUT NOT JUST ANY CHILD, A CHILD WITHOUT A MAN AS A FATHER.

LUCKILY, THERE'S A CONVENIENT PRINCESS WHO CLAIMS THAT A DISAPPEARING DEMON FUCKER (PROBABLY JUST THE BOY NEXT DOOR) IS THE FATHER OF HER CHILD. SHE (SOMEWHAT IRRESPONSIBLY) GIVES THEM HER SON, AN ADORABLE LITTLE KID CALLED MERLIN. YES. THAT MERLIN.

THEY TAKE MERLIN TO SACRIFICE HIM, BUT MERLIN'S SUCH A LITTLE SMART-ASS THAT HE TELLS THEM HOW TO ACTUALLY FIX THE FUCKING CASTLE.

THE SUBSIDENCE IS BEING CAUSED BY A FUCKING GREAT WATER-FILLED HOLE BENEATH THE CASTLE. THEY DRAIN THE WATER OUT AND FIND A COUPLE OF DRAGONS FUCKING AROUND. OF COURSE, THEY BLAME THE FUCKING DRAGONS FOR THE STRUCTURAL DAMAGE. ASSHOLES.

MERLIN IS THE BEST WINGMAN

BEING A MAGICAL LITTLE SHIT, MERLIN IS GENERALLY USEFUL TO HAVE AROUND FOR ANY MINOR PROBLEMS. UTHER PENDRAGON, BRITISH KING WITH BOSS-ASS NAME, FANCIES IGRAINE. BUT SHE'S ALREADY MARRIED TO SOME DUKE MOTHERFUCKER WHO KEEPS HER LOCKED AWAY FROM UTHER AND HIS DICK.

LUCKILY MERLIN IS AROUND, AND HE HELPS UTHER BY MAKING HIM LOOK LIKE IGRAINE'S HUSBAND. SNEAKY.

SO UTHER-IN-CUNNING-DISGUISE FUCKS OFF OVER TO IGRAINE'S AND SLEEPS WITH HER. SUCCESS. NINE MONTHS LATER SHE HAS A CUTE LITTLE SON AND NAMES HIM ARTHUR.

BUT ARTHUR AIN'T NO BASTARD, DON'T FUCKING WORRY. AFTER IGRAINE'S HUSBAND CONVENIENTLY DIES, UTHER MARRIES HER, MAKING ARTHUR HIS LEGIT HEIR.

SO IF YOU NEED HELP GETTING THAT GIRL/GUY/WHOEVER THE FUCK YOU WANT, GIVE MERLIN A SHOUT, HE'S THE KIND OF BRO YOU WANT.

ARTHUR GETS SOME DUMBSHIT SWORD

SINCE MERLIN HAD HELPED UTHER PENDRAGON FUCK HIS CRUSH/FUTURE WIFE IGRAINE, UTHER PROMISES TO GIVE THE RESULTANT BABY TO EVERYONE'S FAVOURITE WIZARD. WHY THE FUCK WOULD YOU JUST GIVE A CHILD TO A STRANGE WIZARD MAN WHY.

LUCKILY MERLIN DOESN'T DO ANY WIZARD FUCKERY TO THE BABY, HE JUST GIVES IT TO SOME FUCKER, SIR ECTOR, WHO NAMES IT ARTHUR.

ARTHUR GROWS UP WITH ECTOR AND NOBODY TELLS HIM HE'S ADOPTED, BECAUSE THAT WOULD BE TOO EASY. MEANWHILE, KING UTHER INCONSIDERATELY DIES AND THERE'S A SHIT TONNE OF ANGRY NOBLES ALL WANTING TO BE KING.

MERLIN SAVES THE DAY AGAIN AND TELLS EVERYONE TO HAVE A BIG MEET-UP AT CHRISTMAS BECAUSE SOME EXCITING SHIT IS ABOUT TO GO DOWN. THE EXCITING SHIT IN QUESTION IS A MASSIVE FUCKING ROCK WITH A SHINY SWORD IN IT, WITH "THE FUCKER WHO PICKS THIS UP IS TOTALLY THE KING OF FUCKING ENGLAND" WRITTEN ON IT.

THEY ALSO HAVE A BIG-ASS TOURNAMENT, BECAUSE IT'S YE OLDE TIMES AND WHY THE FUCK NOT.

TONNES OF ASSFUCKS SHOW UP, AND NONE OF THEM CAN LIFT THIS DAMN SWORD, WHAT A FUCKING SURPRISE. SIR ECTOR VISITS THE PARTY WITH HIS REAL SON, KAY, AND ARTHUR.

KAY IS A FUCKING IDIOT AND LEAVES HIS OWN SWORD AT HOME, SO THEY SEND ARTHUR BACK TO FETCH IT. ARTHUR RIDES ALL THE WAY HOME ONLY TO FIND THE ENTIRE HOUSEHOLD HAS FUCKED OFF AND HE HASN'T A CLUE WHERE KAY'S SWORD IS.

BUT WHERE COULD ARTHUR POSSIBLY FIND A SPARE SWORD? MAYBE THAT MASSIVE FUCKING ROCK WITH A SWORD STICKING OUT OF IT? ARTHUR SNEAKS OVER THERE AND CASUALLY PULLS IT OUT AND GIVES IT TO KAY LIKE THE KIND MOTHERFUCKER HE IS.

ARTHUR IS SUCH AN HONEST LITTLE FUCK HE TELLS EVERYONE WHERE HE GOT IT FROM. THEY MAKE HIM PUT IT BACK IN THE STONE AND TAKE IT OUT AGAIN TO PROVE HE'S NOT A CHEATING FUCK, BUT EVENTUALLY THEY AGREE HE'S THE REAL SHIT.

OF COURSE MOST PEOPLE DIDN'T WANT SOME DUMB KID BEING KING, SO EVEN WHEN HE'S EVENTUALLY CROWNED ALL KINDS OF BITCHES TRY TO FIGHT HIM AND EVERYTHING GETS MESSY AND COMPLICATED. BUT AT LEAST HE HAS A BITCHIN' SWORD AND A PET WIZARD.

ARTHUR'S INCEST ADVENTURE

KING ARTHUR IS HAVING A NASTY-ASS WAR WITH A SHIT TONNE OF OTHER KINGS. ONE OF THEM, KING LOT, FOOLISHLY SENDS HIS WIFE AND CHILDREN TO VISIT ARTHUR AND SPY ON HIM.

ARTHUR IS A HORNY BASTARD WITH NO SELF CONTROL, SO SLEEPS WITH LOT'S WIFE AND GETS HER PREGNANT WITH A SON, MORDRED. WHAT ARTHUR DOESN'T KNOW IS THAT HE'S JUST FUCKED HIS SISTER (IN FAIRNESS ARTHUR DOESN'T KNOW THAT HE'S UTHER PENDRAGON'S SECRET LOVE-CHILD).

ARTHUR HAS SOME TRIPPY DREAMS SO HE DECIDES TO DISTRACT HIMSELF WITH SENSELESS MURDER. HE HUNTS CUTE WILDLIFE SO AGGRESSIVELY THAT HE FUCKING KILLS HIS HORSE. ASSHAT. HE GETS ANOTHER HORSE AND CONTINUES TO CHASE BAMBI'S EXTENDED FAMILY UNTIL A BIG FUCKED-UP MONSTER APPEARS.

IT'S GOT A SNAKE/LEOPARD/LION BODY, IS UGLY AS FUCK AND ALSO WOOFS. ARTHUR IS CONFUSED AS FUCK, BUT THEN A RANDOM KNIGHT SHOWS UP AND TELLS HIM IT'S A QUESTING BEAST AND TOUGH SHIT ARTHUR ISN'T ALLOWED TO HUNT IT. THE KNIGHT THEN STEALS ARTHUR'S HORSE AND FUCKS OFF.

JUST WHEN ARTHUR'S DAY COULDN'T GET ANY WORSE, MERLIN SHOWS UP AND TELLS HIM HE'S SLEPT WITH HIS SISTER AND THE SON HE MADE WILL DESTROY HIM. BALLS.

ARTHUR IS A CARELESS FUCK WITH HIS POSSESSIONS

SOME INJURED MOTHERFUCKER SHOWS UP AT ARTHUR'S COURT, BITCHING ABOUT AN ASSHOLE KNIGHT WHO KILLED HIS MASTER. ARTHUR SENDS HIS ADORABLY NAMED FRIEND GRYFFLET TO JOUST WITH THIS ASSHOLE KNIGHT AND TELL HIM TO FUCK OFF.

GRYFFLET IS AS YOUNG AND ADORABLE AS HIS NAME SUGGESTS AND HE'S FUCKING USELESS, HE GOES OUT TO BEAT THIS KNIGHT AND JUST GETS MANGLED AND LIMPS AWAY.

ARTHUR DECIDES TO BEAT THIS FUCKER UP HIMSELF; THIS KNIGHT IS SIR PELLANOR, THE SAME FUCKER WHO STOLE ARTHUR'S HORSE AND WAS GENERALLY AN ASSHOLE.

MERLIN TELLS ARTHUR THAT FIGHTING PELLANOR IS A SHITTY IDEA, BUT WHY THE FUCK WOULD ARTHUR LISTEN TO REASON. ARTHUR GOES TO FIGHT AND GETS THE CRAP BEATEN OUT OF HIM. HE ALSO CARELESSLY BREAKS HIS FANCY-ASS SWORD, YEAH, THE ONE FROM THE FUCKING STONE.

ARTHUR IS ABOUT TO BE BEHEADED, BUT THEN MERLIN SAVES THE DAY WITH MAGIC (WHAT ELSE IS A PET WIZARD GOOD FOR). MERLIN TELLS ARTHUR TO PLAY NICE WITH SIR PELLANOR BECAUSE IN THE FUTURE HE'LL BE A COOL DUDE.

MERLIN ALSO TAKES ARTHUR DOWN TO A MAGIC LAKE TO GET ANOTHER MAGIC SWORD. A WEIRD MAGIC LADY WAVES A SHINY SWORD OUT OF THE LAKE, AND SAYS ARTHUR CAN HAVE IT IF HE PROMISES HER AN UNSPECIFIED GIFT. BECAUSE THAT DOESN'T SOUND LIKE A REALLY SHITTY IDEA.

ALONG WITH THE SWORD, ARTHUR GETS A MAGIC SCABBARD THAT MAKES HIM INVULNERABLE, AS IF HE NEEDED TO BE ANY MORE OF A SPECIAL SNOWFLAKE.

ARTHUR IS AN ASSHOLE TO CHILDREN

THE HEROIC DICKBAG KING ARTHUR HAS SUDDENLY BECOME WORRIED ABOUT A LITTLE BABY.

THIS LITTLE BABY IS MORDRED, ARTHUR'S SON BY HIS SISTER. MERLIN TOLD HIM THIS INCEST BABY WILL ONE DAY FUCK HIM UP, SO ARTHUR'S CUNNING PLAN TO STOP THIS IS TO KILL ALLLLLL OF THE MOTHERFUCKING BABIES.

HE HAS EVERYONE PUT THEIR BABIES ON A BIG-ASS BOAT AND LETS THE BOAT CRASH INTO SOME ROCKS, AND ALL THE BABIES DROWN. ARTHUR IS A COMPLETE FUCKING ASSHOLE.

OF COURSE, THIS PLAN ULTIMATELY FAILS AND THE ONLY SURVIVING BABY IS MORDRED, WHO IS FOUND AND ADOPTED. WHAT A CUTE INCEST MURDER BABY.

MERLIN GETS A GIRLFRIEND

MERLIN IS A COMPLETE FUCKING IDIOT. FOR ALL THE SENSIBLE ADVICE HE GIVES ARTHUR ABOUT HOW NOT TO FUCK EVERYTHING UP, MERLIN THEN GOES AND FALLS IN LOVE WITH A MYSTERIOUS STRANGE LADY WHO SHOWS UP AT COURT.

HER NAME IS NINEVE, AND SHE ONLY SEEMS TO GIVE A SHIT ABOUT MERLIN BECAUSE SHE WANTS TO LEARN MAGIC FROM HIM. SHE FOLLOWS HIM AROUND FOR A BIT LIKE A CUTE OBSESSIVE GIRLFRIEND, BUT REALLY SHE'S JUST STEALING ALL OF HIS SECRETSSSSS.

ON THE OTHER HAND, NINEVE WON'T SLEEP WITH MERLIN BECAUSE HE'S THE SON OF A FUCKING DEMON. MERLIN SEEMS TO TRUST NINEVE COMPLETELY AND GIVES HER A CUTE TOUR OF INTERESTING PLACES IN BRITAIN.

ONE OF THESE PLACES WAS A CREEPYASS CAVE, SO NINEVE TOOK THE OPPORTUNITY OF TRAPPING HIM IN THE CAVE FOREVER WITH SOME DUMBSHIT SPELL AND FUCKING OFF. WHAT A BITCH.

FEAR FOR YOUR BEARD

TWO BROTHERS, NYNIAW AND PEIBIAW, ARE BEING SHIT-DICKS TO EACH OTHER. INITIALLY THEY'RE ARGUING ABOUT WHO HAS MORE SHEEP AND WHERE TO GRAZE THEM (IT'S WALES, SHEEP ARE SERIOUS BUSINESS), BUT THIS ESCALATES QUICKLY AND THEY START BEATING THE SHIT OUT OF EACH OTHER.

THIS WOULD BE FINE, BUT THESE BROTHERS BOTH HAD MASSIVE ARMIES AND SOON THERE'S A WHOLE FUCKING WAR. SHEEP ARE CLEARLY WORTH IT.

UP IN NORTH-WALES THE GIANT KING RHUDDA GAWR HEARS ABOUT THESE IDIOTS AND THEIR WAR AND THINKS THEY'RE BOTH FUCKING IDIOTS. HE TAKES THE OPPORTUNITY TO ANNIHILATE BOTH SIDES, BECAUSE HE HAS A MASSIVE ARMY AND HE WANTS TO ADD TO HIS BEARD COLLECTION.

RHUDDA HAS A MASSIVE FUCKING CAPE MADE OF THE BEARDS OF HIS ENEMIES. YES, WE WANT ONE TOO.

BY NOW, ALL THE OTHER NEARBY KINGS ARE TERRIFIED FOR THEIR BEARDS SO THE ONLY SOLUTION IS TO KILL RHUDDA AND SAVE THEIR SEXY SEXY FACIAL HAIR. BUT THEY'RE FUCKING USELESS, AND SO RHUDDA BEATS THEM AND ADDS TO HIS BEARD CAPE AND NUMBER OF SHEEP.

ARTHUR SAVES HIS CRAPPY BEARD

KING ARTHUR IS BUSY WIPING GIANT BLOOD OFF HIMSELF FROM HIS FIRST MURDER OF THE DAY WHEN HE HEARS ABOUT SOME GIANT CALLED RHUDDA GAWR WHO'S STEALING BEARDS AND GENERALLY BEING A SHIT-NOZZLE.

RHUDDA DEMANDS ARTHUR'S BEARD FOR HIS COLLECTION AND ALSO HIS LAND. ARTHUR REPLIES, TELLING HIM TO FUCK OFF ABOUT STEALING HIS LAND, BUT HE COULD MAYBE SPARE HIM A BEARD. UNFORTUNATELY ARTHUR'S A KID AT THIS POINT SO HIS BEARD IS PRETTY CRAP AND A FUCKING USELESS GIFT.

BUT RHUDDA GAWR IS A DEMANDING FUCK AND TAKES OFFENCE AT THIS, BRINGING HIS ARMY TO MEET ARTHUR FOR MORE EFFECTIVE BEARD THEFT.

DESPITE HIS EXCELLENT FASHION TASTE, RHUDDA IS A FUCKING IDIOT AND THINKS THE SOUND OF A STORM IS ARTHUR'S ARMY AND THIS SCARES THE SHIT OUT OF HIM. WHEN ARTHUR FINALLY MEETS HIM, HE SUGGESTS THE BEST BEARD FOR RHUDDA'S CAPE WOULD BE HIS OWN.

RHUDDA EVENTUALLY SURRENDERS TO ARTHUR AND ADDS HIS OWN BEARD TO HIS FANCY CLOAK. HE STRUTS AROUND IN THIS FUCKING BEAUTIFUL LOOK UNTIL HE GROWS OLD AND DIES. ALTERNATIVELY ARTHUR MURDERS HIM TO DEATH WHEN THEY MEET.

EITHER WAY, THERE'S NOW A DEAD GIANT AND THIS IS A SERIOUS FUCKING HEALTH AND SAFETY CONCERN. ARTHUR SENDS HIS OWN PEOPLE TO BURY HIM UNDER SOME ROCKS. RHUDDA IS SO FUCKING BIG THAT THIS PILE OF ROCKS BECOMES A FUCKING MOUNTAIN (YR WYDDFA, OR SNOWDON).

SIR LAUNCELOT ENJOYS NAP TIME

SIR LAUNCELOT HAS JUST GOT BACK FROM SUCCESSFUL ADVENTURES IN ROME AND IS NOW KING ARTHUR'S FUCKING FAVOURITE KNIGHT. WHAT AN ASS-LICKER.

BUT LAUNCELOT CAN'T JUST LEAVE IT AT THAT, SO HE SETS OUT FROM CAMELOT FOR ANOTHER KNIGHTLY ADVENTURE WITH HIS BRO SIR LIONEL. BUT LAUNCELOT IS A USELESS FUCK AND NOT LONG INTO THE ADVENTURE HE NEEDS A FUCKING NAP.

WHILE LAUNCELOT SLEEPS, LIONEL IS A COMPLETE FUCKHEAD AND GOES TO INVESTIGATE SOME MEAN-LOOKING KNIGHT WHO HAS BEEN KIDNAPPING PUNIER KNIGHTS. BUT LIONEL IS ALSO A BIT OF A PUNY KNIGHT AND GETS HIMSELF KIDNAPPED TOO.

THEY'RE DRAGGED BACK TO A ~~KINKY SEX~~ DUNGEON, STRIPPED NAKED AND BEATEN WITH THORNS. BECAUSE WHY THE FUCK NOT.

MEANWHILE LAUNCELOT IS STILL SLEEPING WHEN FOUR LADIES RIDE UP TO HIM. LAUNCELOT IS SEXY AS FUCK SO THEY ALL IMMEDIATELY FALL IN LOVE WITH HIM. UNFORTUNATELY, ONE OF THESE LADIES IS ARTHUR'S EVIL MAGIC SISTER MORGAN LE FAY, AND SHE IMMEDIATELY DECIDES TO JUST KIDNAP THIS ATTRACTIVE UNCONSCIOUS STRANGER. WHAT A FUCKING CREEP.

THE GIRLS TAKE LAUNCELOT BACK TO THEIR CASTLE AND TELL HIM TO PICK HIS FAVOURITE OF THEM OR FUCKING DIE. THESE ARE SOME CRAZY LADIES YEAH. HE TELLS THEM TO FUCK OFF AND ESCAPES.

ON HIS JOURNEY AWAY FROM THE CASTLE OF HORNY LADIES, LAUNCELOT GETS SLEEPY AGAIN. CONVENIENTLY, HE FINDS A NICE TENT WITH A BED MADE UP IN IT. IT'S CLEARLY NOT A GREAT FUCKING IDEA, BUT LAUNCELOT SLEEPS THERE ANYWAY.

SOMETIME IN THE NIGHT, THE OWNER OF THE TENT APPEARS AND GETS INTO HIS BED, THINKING LAUNCELOT IS HIS FUCKING

GIRLFRIEND. THEY END UP SPOONING AND IT'S FUCKING AWKWARD, SO WHEN LAUNCELOT REALISES, HE BEATS THE SHIT OUT OF THIS STRANGER. THIS SEEMS TO BE THE COMPLETE NORM IN ARTHURIAN TIMES. WE APPROVE.

SURPRISE BABIES

MATH IS A CRAZY WELSH GOD WHO CAN ONLY SLEEP IF HE'S RESTING HIS FEET ON THE LAP OF A VIRGIN. WHAT A DEMANDING FUCKER. ONE DAY HIS FOOTSTOOL VIRGIN GETS KIDNAPPED, SO HE CAN'T SLEEP. IT'S A FUCKING DISASTER.

HIS NEPHEW GWYDION HAS AN IDEA. HE OFFERS MATH HIS SISTER ARIANRHOD AS A NEW FOOTSTOOL, BECAUSE OBVIOUSLY SHE'S A FUCKING VIRGIN. AS SOON AS SHE SITS DOWN TO START HER NEW JOB AS A STOOL, THOUGH, TWO BABIES FALL OUT OF HER. HOW THE FUCK DID THEY GET THERE? OBVIOUSLY SHE'S NOT A FUCKING VIRGIN, BUT BABIES DON'T USUALLY JUST FALL OUT OF PEOPLE. EVERYONE IGNORES HER DISTURBING ANATOMICAL ISSUES, THOUGH, AND TRIES TO WORK OUT WHAT THE FUCK TO DO WITH THE BABIES. THE FIRST SON, KNOWN AS DYLAN EIL TON, HURLS HIMSELF OUT OF HIS MOTHERS ARMS AND INTO THE SEA, BECAUSE HE'S A CRAZY FUCKER. GWYDION HAS A PLAN FOR THE SECOND CHILD, AND STEALS HIM. BABY NUMBER TWO IS RAISED IN A WOODEN CHEST, AND GROWS UP TO BE LLEU LLAW GYFFES, WHO HAS ALL SORTS OF FUCKING WEIRD ADVENTURES.

FLOWER FACE AND THE HOT KNIGHT

THERE'S A WELSH WIZARD WOMAN CALLED ARIANRHOD, WHO HAS A BABY. IT'S HER SECOND BABY, BUT SHE'S HAD ENOUGH, BECAUSE THE FIRST ONE'S A LITTLE SHIT. BECAUSE SHE'S FUCKING VINDICTIVE AND A SHIT PARENT, SHE CURSES HIM TO NEVER HAVE A NAME ANYONE BUT HER GIVES HIM, AND THEN SHE CALLS HIM LLEU LLAW GYFFES. THAT'S JUST FUCKING CRUEL.

BECAUSE THAT'S NOT CRUEL ENOUGH FOR HER AND SHE'S A REALLY SHIT PARENT, SHE CURSES HIM AGAIN. THIS TIME, THAT NOBODY EXCEPT HER COULD EVER GIVE HIM ARMOUR. THEN SHE REALISES THAT'S A SHIT CURSE AND TRIES AGAIN. THIS TIME, SHE CURSES HIM TO NEVER MARRY A MORTAL WOMAN. HER PARENTING REALLY IS FUCKING TERRIBLE.

FORTUNATELY, WALES IS FULL OF WIZARDS. WIZARDS AND FUCKING SHEEP. OCCASIONALLY WIZARDS FUCKING SHEEP. THE WIZARDS DON'T WANT TO SHARE THE SHEEP, SO THEY DECIDE TO GET LLEU A WOMAN.

THE CRAZY WIZARDS MAKE A WOMAN OUT OF FLOWERS, AND THEY CALL HER BLODEUWEDD, WHICH MEANS "FLOWER FACE". WIZARDS HAVE NO FUCKING IMAGINATION. FORTUNATELY, LLEU FALLS IN LOVE WITH FLOWER FACE, DESPITE THE FACT THAT SHE'S MADE OF STICKS, AND THEY GET MARRIED.

UNFORTUNATELY, SHE HAS AN AFFAIR WITH THE FIRST HOT KNIGHT TO COME PAST THE CASTLE WHILE LLEU IS OUT. FLOWER FACE DECIDES TO MURDER LLEU SO SHE CAN RUN AWAY WITH THE HOT KNIGHT, AND JUST OUTRIGHT ASKS HIM HOW HE COULD BE KILLED. TURNS OUT HE'S MAGIC AND CAN ONLY BE KILLED WHEN HE'S ABOUT TO HAVE A BATH. AND WHEN HE HAS ONE FOOT ON THE BATH AND ONE ON A MOTHERFUCKING GOAT. AND WHEN HE'S NEITHER INDOORS OR OUTDOORS. OH, AND HE CAN ONLY BE KILLED BY A SPEAR THAT TOOK EXACTLY A YEAR TO MAKE. IT'S ALL FUCKING RIDICULOUS, BUT THAT KNIGHT WAS REALLY HOT, SO FLOWER FACE GETS TO WORK.

FLOWER FACE TELLS THE HOT KNIGHT, AND HE BELIEVES ALL THIS RIDICULOUS BULLSHIT. THE HOT KNIGHT IS A GULLIBLE FUCK, BUT IT'S ALL TRUE THIS TIME. HE MAKES HIS SPEAR AND SETS UP A PILE OF GOATS AND A BATH UNDER THE EDGE OF A ROOF. IT'S CONTRIVED AS FUCK, BUT FORTUNATELY FOR HIM LLEU IS FUCKING STUPID. HE STANDS ON THE GOAT, AND THE HOT KNIGHT STABS HIM IN THE FACE WITH A SPEAR.

LLEU DOESN'T DIE THOUGH, BECAUSE HE'S FUCKING MAGICAL. INSTEAD, HE TURNS INTO A MOTHERFUCKING EAGLE AND FLIES AWAY. EVENTUALLY HE TURNS BACK INTO A MAN AND SETS OUT FOR REVENGE.

HE STABS THE HOT KNIGHT IN THE FACE (HE DOESN'T TURN INTO A MAGICAL FUCKING EAGLE BECAUSE HE'S NOT FUCKING MAGIC) AND THEN TURNS FLOWER FACE INTO AN OWL BECAUSE OWLS ARE FUCKING SCARY AND NOBODY WILL LOVE HER AGAIN.

SHITTY WELSH BOYFRIENDS

ONE DAY, SOME FUCKER CALLED MAELON DYFODRULL COMES TO VISIT THE CASTLE OF KING BRYCHAN BRYCHEINIOG, WHO'S SOME SORT OF IRISH IMMIGRANT. BRYCHAN IS A HORNY BASTARD WITH THIRTY-SIX FUCKING DAUGHTERS.

ONE OF HIS DAUGHTERS, DWYNWEN, FALLS IN LOVE WITH MAELON, BUT BRYCHAN ISN'T HAVING ANY OF THAT SHIT. HE WANTS TO KEEP HIS DAUGHTER COLLECTION, SO HE TELLS MAELON TO FUCK OFF AND LEAVE HIS DAUGHTER ALONE.

DWYNWEN RUNS AWAY FROM HOME, AND MAELON FUCKS OFF AFTER HER. HE CATCHES UP TO HER, AND SHE TELLS HIM TO FUCK OFF TOO BECAUSE SHE DOESN'T WANT TO PISS HER FATHER OFF ANY MORE. HE'S PRETTY FUCKING ANGRY ABOUT THIS AND THREATENS TO RAPE HER, BECAUSE HE'S A FUCKING DICK, AND SHE PRAYS FOR HELP.

WHEN SHE OPENS HER EYES, MAELON HAS TURNED INTO A FUCKING SNOWMAN. SHE REALISES THAT CLEARLY GOD WILL GIVE HER WHAT SHE ASKS FOR, SO DECIDES TO FUCK ABOUT WITH THAT FOR A BIT. SHE WISHES TO BE FREE FROM MAELON, BECAUSE HE'S A DICK. THAT'S FINE, SHE'S ALREADY HAD HIM TURNED INTO A SNOWMAN; HE'S NOT GOING TO BE BOTHERING HER AGAIN. THEN SHE WISHES TO NEVER MARRY ANYONE. THAT'S NOT REALLY SOMETHING SHE NEEDED TO WISH FOR, BUT WHATEVER. FINALLY, SHE WISHES TO BE ALLOWED TO HELP COUPLES. THEN SHE FUCKS OFF TO BE A TRAVELLING RELATIONSHIP COUNSELLOR AND RAPIST-FREEZER, WHICH IS A PRETTY FUCKING UNIQUE JOB.

DRAGONS IN A BLANKET

LONDON IS FULL OF FUCKING AWFUL NOISES, AND NOBODY IN THE ENTIRE FUCKING CITY CAN GET ANY SLEEP AT ALL. EVERYTHING IS SHIT, AND KING LLUDD SETS OUT TO FIX THIS STUPID BULLSHIT SO HE CAN GO TO BED.

HE GOES TO ASK HIS BROTHER LLEFELYS WHAT THE FUCK IS GOING ON, BECAUSE LLEFELYS IS A CRAZY-ASS WIZARD AND REALLY FUCKING GOOD AT MAKING PEOPLE SHUT THE HELL UP.

LLEFELYS TELLS HIM WHAT THE PROBLEM IS. IT'S MOTHERFUCKING DRAGONS FIGHTING. THERE'S A FUCKING MASSIVE ENGLISH DRAGON AND A FUCKING MASSIVE WELSH DRAGON, AND THEY'RE BEATING THE SHIT OUT OF EACH OTHER AND SHOUTING A LOT.

LLEFELYS TELLS LLUDD WHAT TO DO, AND HE SETS OUT TO MAKE THE DRAGONS SHUT THE FUCK UP. HE FINDS THE EXACT CENTRE OF BRITAIN, DIGS A FUCKING MASSIVE HOLE, AND FILLS IT WITH MEAD. THEN HE PUTS A BLANKET OVER IT TO HIDE THE HOLE. WHEN THEY GET TIRED, THE DRAGONS FLY TO THE HOLE, MAGICALLY TRANSFORM INTO FUCKING ADORABLE PIGLETS, AND SIT ON THE BLANKET, AT WHICH POINT THEY FALL INTO THE MEAD. WHEN THEY'VE DRUNKEN THE MEAD, THE DRAGONS ARE STUCK IN THE FORM OF SMALL DRUNK PIGLETS, AND LLUDD CAN JUST ROLL THEM UP IN THE BLANKET AND BURY THEM IN A SHITTY FIELD SOMEWHERE. FIGHTING DRAGONS IS MUCH EASIER WHEN THEY'RE ACTUALLY JUST DRUNK PIGLETS.

A PLAGUE OF WIZARDS

LONDON IS OVERRUN WITH A PLAGUE. NOT A PLAGUE OF PLAGUE OR A PLAGUE OF RATS OR FROGS OR WHICHEVER BULLSHIT ANIMALS MOST PLAGUES ARE MADE OF, BUT A PLAGUE OF EVIL WIZARDS. THEY'RE CALLED THE CORANIEID, AND THEY STAND AROUND IN BIG-ASS BLACK CLOAKS LOOKING THREATENING. ALSO THEY CAN HEAR EVERY SINGLE WORD ANYONE SAYS, SO THEY LISTEN TO EVERYONE'S SECRETS AND USE THEM TO FUCK SHIT UP. ONCE AGAIN, KING LUDD IS FED UP WITH THIS STUPID BULLSHIT AND SETS OUT TO BEAT THE SHIT OUT OF THE CORANIEID.

LLUDD PHONES UP HIS WIZARD BROTHER LLEFELYS ON THEIR SPECIAL COPPER SPEAKING TUBE SO THAT THE CORANIEID CAN'T HEAR THEIR PLOTS, BUT UNFORTUNATELY THE PHONE LINE IS CLOGGED WITH EVIL DEMONS. LLUDD POURS A BOTTLE OF WINE INTO THE PHONE, AND THE DEMONS GET WASHED OUT OF THE OTHER END, LEAVING LLEFELYS WITH A PILE OF WET, WINE-STAINED DEMONS TO DEAL WITH.

ONCE HE'S SWEPT UP THE DEMONS AND CLEANED THE FLOOR, LLEFELY TELLS LLUDD WHAT TO DO. THE CORANIEID ARE IMMUNE TO NORMAL WEAPONS, WHICH IS A PRETTY FUCKING MASSIVE PROBLEM. FORTUNATELY, THOUGH, THEY HAVE ONE WEAKNESS. BEES.

LLUDD GRINDS UP HUNDREDS OF FUCKING BEES AND SPRAYS THE CORANIEID WITH BEE JUICE, AT WHICH POINT THEY DIE AN AGONISING MELTY BEE DEATH. IT'S FUCKING HORRIBLE, BUT AT LEAST LONDON ISN'T PLAGUED WITH EVIL WIZARDS ANY MORE.

SCOTTISH MYTHOLOGY

ACTUAL CANNIBAL SEAN BEAN

YOUNG SCOTTISH FUCKER, SAWNEY BEAN (LET'S JUST CALL HIM SEAN BEAN OK, MOTHERFUCKERS) LEAVES HOME AND GETS HIMSELF A WIFE. ISN'T THAT FUCKING ADORABLE. THEY GO OUT AND LIVE IN A CAVE BECAUSE CAVES ARE FUCKING SUPERIOR LAIRS.

INSTEAD OF GETTING A JOB LIKE A REASONABLE MOTHERFUCKER, MR AND MRS BEAN LIKE TO MURDER TRAVELLERS AND STEAL ALL OF THEIR NICE SHIT. THIS IS GREAT BUT WHAT TO DO WITH A FUCKTONNE OF CORPSES? EAT THEM. EAT ALL OF THE DEAD PEOPLE.

THEY HAVE SO MANY CORPSES TO EAT THAT THEY SOMETIMES HAVE TO THROW OUT LEFTOVERS, AND THE LOCALS GET A LITTLE SUSPICIOUS. BUT THE LOCALS ARE ALL FUCKING IDIOTS AND DO FUCK ALL ABOUT IT.

ALL THIS CANNIBAL FUCKERY CONTINUES FOR YEARS AND SOON THERE ARE MANY BEAN CHILDREN. THEN A SHIT TONNE OF INCEST HAPPENS AND THERE ARE EVEN MORE LITTLE BEANS.

THEN FINALLY THE BEAN FAMILY FUCKS UP; THEY CATCH A MAN AND HIS WIFE AND ARE SO BUSY DRINKING HER BLOOD THAT THE MAN MANAGES TO GET AWAY AND SOON THERE'S A WHOLE FUCKING ARMY SENT AFTER HOUSE BEAN.

SEAN BEAN AND HIS SONS HAVE THEIR LIMBS CHOPPED OFF AND ARE LEFT TO BLEED TO DEATH; THE LADIES ARE BURNED BECAUSE FIRE IS FUN.

MORAL OF THE STORY; HIDE YOUR CANNIBALISM A LITTLE BETTER NEXT TIME. ALSO DON'T BE SEAN BEAN. IT DOESN'T FUCKING END WELL.

KELPIES DON'T KNOW SHIT ABOUT FIRE

THE KELPIE IN LOCH GARVE REALLY FUCKING LIKES HIS COLD DARK CORNER OF THE LOCH. UNFORTUNATELY HIS KELPIE WIFE IS A COMPLETE WIMP AND KEEPS BITCHING ABOUT HOW FUCKING COLD IT IS.

TO SOLVE THIS SHIT, MR KELPIE GOES OUT ONTO LAND DISGUISED AS A HOT, HOT HORSE. THIS SHIT WORKS EVERY TIME. HE FINDS A BUILDER FUCKING STUPID ENOUGH TO CLIMB ONTO HIS BACK AND KIDNAPS THIS IDIOT AND TAKES HIM BACK TO THE LOCH.

THE BUILDER DOESN'T HAVE A CLUE WHAT'S GOING ON AND JUST FUCKING ROLLS WITH IT WHEN MR KELPIE TELLS HIM TO BUILD A FIREPLACE FOR HIS WIFE. A FIREPLACE. UNDERWATER. WHY THE FUCK NOT.

SO MRS KELPIE GETS HER FIREPLACE AND NOW SHE'S NICE AND WARM AND ALSO MAYBE ON FIRE. WHO THE FUCK KNOWS. THEY LIVED HAPPILY EVER AFTER THOUGH, WHICH IS FUCKING RARE AS SHIT.

MICHAEL SCOTT STEALS SNAKE JUICE

MICHAEL SCOTT (PROBABLY NOT THE CLASSICIST OR THAT FUCKER FROM THE OFFICE, BUT WE LIVE IN HOPE) IS A BADASS SCOTTISH MAGIC FUCKER.

MICHAEL GETS HIS MAGIC POWERS FROM SOME FUCKERY INVOLVING A GIANT SNAKE. IT'S ALWAYS GOT TO BE SNAKES. YOUNG MICHAEL IS PISSING AROUND ON AN ADVENTURE AND BEATS A LARGE SNAKE TO DEATH SO FUCKING BADLY IT BREAKS INTO THREE PIECES.

SOME CRAZY OLD LADY (REPUTABLE SOURCE) TELLS HIM THIS SNAKE IS A MAGICAL DICKSHIT WHO WILL COME BACK TO LIFE IF MICHAEL DOESN'T REMOVE ITS MIDDLE SECTION. SO HE GOES BACK TO THE SCENE OF THE BRUTAL MURDER AND PICKS UP THE SNAKE LUMP.

THERE'S NO PROPER WAY TO DISPOSE OF A SNAKE LUMP OTHER THAN JUST FUCKING EATING THE EVIDENCE, SO THE NICE OLD LADY MAKES A BIG FUCKING SNAKE STEW AND TELLS MICHAEL TO LOOK AFTER IT.

MICHAEL IS FUCKING USELESS AT TEMPTATION AND STEALS A TASTE OF THE SNAKE STEW FIRST. THE OLD LADY IS SUPER FUCKING MAD AT HIM FOR THIS, BECAUSE NOW HE HAS MAGIC POWERS FROM THE SNAKE JUICE.

DESPITE BEING SCREWED OVER HERE SHE'S STILL QUITE HAPPY AS SNAKE STEW IS DAMN GOOD. MICHAEL SCOTT FUCKS OFF FOR FURTHER WIZARD FUCKERY.

HE THEN GETS SO MANY MAGIC MINIONS THAT HE HAS TO GIVE THEM ALL BULLSHIT JOBS TO KEEP THEM BUSY. EVENTUALLY HE TELLS THEM TO FUCK OFF AND BUILD A LADDER TO THE MOON BECAUSE THAT'S REALLY WHAT THIRTEENTH CENTURY SCOTLAND WAS LACKING.

PASSIVE-AGGRESSIVE MERMAID

A MAN AND HIS WIFE LIVE IN SOME CUTE LITTLE COTTAGE BY THE SEA. HE'S A FUCKING IDIOT AND DOESN'T NOTICE THERE'S A MERMAID WHO LIKES TO HANG OUT ON A ROCK NEARBY, BECAUSE SHE ONLY SINGS AT NIGHT AND HE'S A DEEP SLEEPER.

WHEN THEY HAVE A BABY THE LITTLE SHIT WON'T STOP CRYING AT NIGHT AND THE WHOLE FAMILY ARE ANGRY AND CONFUSED (A NATURAL REACTION TO A NOISY BIRTHLING).EVENTUALLY THEY REALISE THAT THE BABY IS CRYING BECAUSE THEIR FUCKING FRIENDLY NEIGHBOURHOOD MERMAID WON'T SHUT THE FUCK UP WHEN BITCHES ARE TRYING TO SLEEP.

THE FATHER SENDS SOMEONE TO TELL HER, VERY POLITELY, TO SHUT THE FUCK UP. SHE TELLS HIM TO FUCK OFF AND KEEPS SINGING, BUT THIS TIME HER SINGING IS EVEN LOUDER AND MORE ANNOYING.

SHE IS REPEATEDLY ASKED TO SHUT UP BUT KEEPS SINGING LOUDER, UNTIL EVENTUALLY THE FAMILY GO OUT AND DESTROY THE MERMAID'S FAVOURITE CHILL-OUT SPOT BECAUSE THEY ARE A COMPLETE BUNCH OF DICKS.

THE MERMAID KEEPS SINGING. THEN SHE GETS INTO SCREAMO SHIT AND SCREAMS SO FUCKING LOUD THAT THE BABY DIES. DON'T ANGER MERMAIDS THEY ARE VINDICTIVE SHITS.

THE GOODMAN O' WASTNESS IS REALLY JUST A DICK

THIS GOODMAN IS A HANDSOME YOUNG FUCKER, AND ALL THE LOCAL GIRLS WANT TO TAP THAT. BUT HE'S TOO FULL OF HIS "HOLIER THAN THOU" BULLSHIT AND WON'T CONSIDER MARRYING ANY OF THEM BECAUSE HE THINKS WOMEN TURN EVERYTHING TO SHIT. HE'S AN ASSHOLE, BASICALLY.

ONE DAY HE GOES FOR A WALK ON THE BEACH AND SEES A BUNCH OF NAKED PEOPLE PLAYING ON THE BEACH. THIS IS CLEARLY NOT A NUDIST BEACH AS THESE NAKED FUCKERS ARE ALL YOUNG AND SEXY.

THEY HAVE A BUNCH OF SEAL SKINS LYING IN A PILE, AND GOODMAN REALISES THAT THIS IS SOME MAGIC SELKIE SHIT GOING DOWN. SELKIES ARE LIKE WERE-SEALS, AND ARE GENERALLY SUPER HOT AND SUPER NICE. SO GOODMAN DECIDES TO BE A COMPLETE TWAT AND RUN OVER TO THEM AND FUCK SHIT UP.

HE GRABS ONE OF THE SKINS AND ALL THE SELKIES JUMP BACK INTO THE SEA AND TURN BACK INTO SEALS. SEXY NAKED SEALS. EXCEPT ONE, WHO HAS TO STAY HUMAN BECAUSE HE STOLE HER FUCKING SEAL SKIN AND HID IT. NOT FUCKING COOL MAN. EVENTUALLY THE SELKIE GIRL FOLLOWS HIM TO HIS HOUSE AND BEGS FOR HER FUCKING SKIN BACK. HE SAYS FUCK NO AND FORCES HER TO MARRY HIM, BECAUSE HE'S DECIDED SHE'S THE ONLY WOMAN GOOD ENOUGH FOR HIM.

THIS KIDNAP BULLSHIT LASTS FOR YEARS AND THEY HAVE A WHOLE POD OF CHILDREN. THE SELKIE KEEPS ASKING FOR HER SKIN AND HER FREEDOM BACK BUT GOODMAN REMAINS A DICK. EVENTUALLY ONE OF THEIR KIDS SEES HIM TAKE THE SKIN OUT OF ITS HIDING PLACE TO MAKE OUT WITH IT OR SOME BULLSHIT LIKE THAT. THE KID TELLS THEIR MOTHER WHERE IT IS, SHE TAKES IT AND FUCKS OFF BACK TO THE SEA TO BE WITH HER SELKIE FAMILY AND HER SELKIE HUSBAND.

SERIOUSLY DON'T STEAL PEOPLE'S CLOTHES/SKINS/PASSPORTS/WHATEVER. THERE ARE BETTER WAYS OF GETTING A DATE, MOTHERFUCKERS.

FAIRIES WANT YOUR BABIES

SOMEWHERE IN SCOTLAND, A PIG IS SICK. HER OWNER IS A SINGLE MOTHER AND ONLY HAS ONE PIG. THIS IS FUCKING UPSETTING BECAUSE WITHOUT A PIG HER LIFE WOULD BE SAD AND LACKING IN BACON.

THE WOMAN CRIES ABOUT HER PIG FOR A BIT, BUT THEN A MYSTERIOUS FAIRY LADY SHOWS UP, NOT LOOKING FUCKING SUSPICIOUS AT ALL. THE WOMAN SAYS SHE WOULD GIVE THE FAIRY ANYTHING TO SAVE HER PIG. THE FAIRY WANTS HER BABY (PRESUMABLY FOR EATING PURPOSES).

SEEMINGLY THE WOMAN IS COOL WITH SWAPPING THE BABY FOR A PIG BECAUSE BACON IS MORE IMPORTANT AND THEY MAKE THE DEAL. IN SOME BULLSHIT FAIRY LEGAL LOOPHOLE, THE WOMAN CAN GET HER BABY BACK IF SHE GUESSES THE FAIRY'S NAME WITHIN THREE DAYS.

AFTER TWO DAYS GOING THROUGH ALL THE OBVIOUS NAMES LIKE RUMPLESTILTSKIN, TOM TIT TOT AND NIGEL, THE WOMAN GIVES UP AND GOES FOR A WALK IN THE WOODS. IN SOME BULLSHIT PLOT TWIST, THE FAIRY IS SITTING IN A QUARRY SINGING ABOUT HERSELF.

HER NAME IS WHUPPITY STOORIE. WHAT THE ACTUAL FUCK.

THE WOMAN GETS HER BABY BACK AND EVERYONE LIVES HAPPILY EVER AFTER WITH BACON.

IRISH MYTHOLOGY

IRISH HEROES ARE UNPRONOUNCEABLE

IRISH MYTHOLOGY IS MOSTLY LESS FUCKED UP THAN GREEK MYTHOLOGY, BUT IT'S STILL PRETTY FUCKING WEIRD.

THE MOST NOTABLE IRISH HERO IS FIONN MAC CUMHAILL, AND WHO THE FUCK KNOWS HOW TO PRONOUNCE THAT? FUCKING NOBODY, THAT'S WHO.

FIONN'S FATHER IS A DICK WHO MANAGED TO GET HIMSELF EXILED, SO FIONN'S STUCK OUT IN THE WILDS OF IRELAND, WHERE THEY HAVE NOTHING BUT ALCOHOL AND MONSTERS. IT'S A FUCKING ROUGH LIFE FOR A KID.

HE'S RAISED IN THE MAGIC FOREST, AND ONE DAY HE MEETS A LEPRECHAUN CALLED FINNECHAS. FOR SOME REASON HE DECIDES TO TRUST THE LEPRECHAUN, WHO TELLS HIM TO FUCK OFF AND CATCH THE MAGIC SALMON OF KNOWLEDGE. FIONN DOESN'T QUESTION WHY THE MAGIC MIDGET IN THE FOREST WANTS HIM TO CATCH A MAGIC FISH, AND GOES OFF TO DEAL WITH IT. FIONN CATCHES THE MAGIC FISH AND COOKS IT, INTENDING TO GIVE IT TO FINNECHAS, WHO HAS BEEN TRYING TO CATCH THE SLIMY FUCKER FOR SEVEN YEARS. WHOEVER EATS THE MAGIC FISH WILL GET ALL THE KNOWLEDGE IN THE ENTIRE WORLD.

FIONN BURNS HIS HAND TRYING TO COOK THE FISH, AND STICKS HIS THUMB IN HIS MOUTH TO TRY TO STOP HURTING. FORTUNATELY FOR HIM, HE HAS A BIT OF FISH ON HIS HAND, SO ACCIDENTALLY EATS PART OF THE MAGIC FISH, GIVING HIM AN ENORMOUS AMOUNT OF KNOWLEDGE. BUT ONLY WHEN HE SUCKS HIS THUMB.

HE'S THE GREATEST HERO IN IRELAND, AND HE CAN SOLVE ALL HIS PROBLEMS BY SUCKING HIS FUCKING THUMB. WHAT THE FUCK.

MOTHERFUCKING ARSON FAIRIES

ONCE A YEAR AT THE END OF OCTOBER, SOME CRAZY MOTHERFUCKING FAIRY CALLED AILLEN (THAT'S RIGHT, THERE'S A FAIRY CALLED ALAN) SHOWS UP AT THE PALACE OF TARA. AILLEN IS A COMPLETE FUCKING PSYCHO AND CAN ALSO BREATHE FIRE. EVERY YEAR, HE SHOWS UP, MAGICS EVERYONE TO SLEEP, AND BURNS THE FUCKING PALACE TO THE GROUND, AND NOBODY CAN DO SHIT ABOUT IT BECAUSE HE'S A MOTHERFUCKING FAIRY.

FORTUNATELY, FIONN THE MAGIC THUMB SUCKER IS ON THE CASE. HE SHOWS UP WITH HIS FATHER'S BAG OF MAGIC WEAPONS TO BEAT THE SHIT OUT OF THE FAIRY. IN ORDER TO STOP HIMSELF FROM BEING MAGICKED TO SLEEP, HE STABS HIMSELF IN THE FACE WITH HIS SPEAR SO THE PAIN KEEPS HIM AWAKE. FIONN IS A CRAZY MOTHERFUCKER.

IT TURNS OUT THAT IF YOU'RE NOT ASLEEP, IT'S FUCKING EASY TO KILL A FAIRY, EVEN IF IT BREATHES FIRE. FIONN IS BLEEDING OUT OF HIS FACE AND THEREFORE NOT ASLEEP, SO HE JUST STABS AILLEN THE ARSON FAIRY TILL HE DIES.

FIONN FUCKS A DEER

ONE DAY, A DRUID CALLED FEAR DOIRICH (THE MOST EVIL NAME POSSIBLE) ASKS A WOMAN CALLED SADHBH (ONCE AGAIN, FUCKING UNPRONOUNCEABLE) TO MARRY HIM. SHE SAYS NO, BECAUSE HE'S A CREEPY MOTHERFUCKER AND OBVIOUSLY EVIL, SO HE TURNS HER INTO A DEER. WHAT A FUCKING DICK.

SOME TIME LATER, FIONN GOES OUT HUNTING WITH HIS MAGIC DOGS THAT USED TO BE PEOPLE, AND SPOTS SADHBH THE MAGIC DEER. INSTEAD OF SHOOTING HER, HE'S AMAZED BY JUST HOW FUCKING HOT THAT DEER IS, AND TAKES HER HOME WITH HIM. DIRTY BASTARD.

AS SOON AS SHE STEPS OVER THE BOUNDARY INTO HIS LAND, SHE TURNS BACK INTO A PERSON, SO HE FUCKS HER. OF COURSE, EVERY TIME SHE LEAVES HIS LAND SHE TURNS BACK INTO A DEER, SO SHE'S TRAPPED IN HIS HOUSE, UNABLE TO LEAVE. SHE'S BASICALLY HIS SEX SLAVE. EVERYONE IN IRELAND IS A DICK.

HAIRY MONSTERS ARE FUCKING STUPID

FIONN'S JUST SITTING THERE SUCKING HIS THUMB AND DOING FUCK ALL WITH HIS LIFE WHEN HE SUDDENLY REALISES THERE'S A BUGGANE COMING TO HIS HOUSE TO BEAT THE SHIT OUT OF HIM. BUGGANES ARE HAIRY GIANTS THAT LIVE UNDERGROUND AND HAVE HUGE CLAWS AND TUSKS. BASICALLY GIANT TALKING MURDER-MOLES.

FIONN DECIDES TO PLAY A CRUEL TRICK ON THE BUGGANE, BECAUSE HE'S A DICK. HE DRESSES UP AS A BABY AND GETS INTO BED, AFTER PERSUADING HIS WIFE TO MAKE FUCKLOADS OF CAKES AND HIDE FRYING PANS IN SOME OF THEM.

THE BUGGANE SHOWS UP TO BEAT THE SHIT OUT OF FIONN, AND IS TOLD THAT FIONN'S OUT AT THE MOMENT BUT HE'S WELCOME TO STICK AROUND AND HAVE SOME CAKE.

THE BUGGANE TAKES ONE OF THE CAKES AND BITES INTO IT, BUT THE FRYING PAN BREAKS HIS TEETH. WHILE THE BUGGANE IS NURSING HIS BROKEN FACE, FIONN (STILL DRESSED UP AS A BABY) TAKES ONE OF THE NORMAL CAKES AND EATS IT. THE BUGGANE, NOT SUSPECTING THAT THE 6 FOOT BEARDED BABY MIGHT NOT ACTUALLY BE A BABY, IS SCARED SHITLESS OF HOW EVEN FIONN'S BABY CAN BITE THROUGH SUCH HARD CAKES. CLEARLY IT THINKS THE BABY HAS RAZORS FOR TEETH OR SOME SHIT LIKE THAT. TERRIFIED OF THE KILLER BABY, IT RUNS AWAY AND IS NEVER SEEN AGAIN.

THE MORAL OF THAT STORY IS THAT IF SOMEONE IS COMING TO BEAT THE SHIT OUT OF YOU, YOU SHOULD JUST DRESS UP AS A BABY AND PLAY TRICKS ON THEM. BABIES ARE FUCKING SCARY.

MORE CRAP CHILD-CARE

LIR IS A KING/SEA-GOD/GENERAL FUCKER IN IRISH/CELTIC MYTH. THIS FUCKER HAD A HANDFUL OF CHILDREN, WHICH WASS FUCKING GREAT. THEN HIS WIFE DIED/WENT INTO SOME COMA THING.

EITHER WAY, LIR IS A BIT OF A SHIT AND IMMEDIATELY MARRIES HIS WIFE'S SISTER, AOIFE. SHE SPENDS ALL HER TIME FEELING GUILTY AND ANGRY AT HAVING TO RAISE HER SISTER'S KIDS. SHE GETS SO GRUMPY THAT SHE SUDDENLY BECOMES A SUPER OLD LADY. BALLS.

ONE DAY THE KIDDIES ARE PLAYING IN A LAKE, BEING ALL CUTE AND THAT. EVIL STEP-MOTHER AOIFE IS STANDING ON THE SHORE, MENACING. RUN FUCKERS, RUN. THE KIDS DON'T RUN BECAUSE CLEARLY THEY DIDN'T NOTICE THEIR EVIL WITCHY STEP-MOTHER PUT HER SCARY MAGIC CLOAK ON.

SHE CAN'T KILL THE KIDS, BECAUSE THAT WOULD BE FUCKING BORING. SO INSTEAD SHE EITHER HITS THEM WITH HER WAND, OR CHUCKS A MASSIVE MOTHERFUCKING FIRESTORM AT THEM FOR MAGICAL SHENANIGANS.

AIOFE TELLS LIR THAT THE KIDS WERE MYSTERIOUSLY ALL KILLED BY WILD BOARS. HOW FUCKING SAD. BUT REALLY, SHE HAD TURNED THEM INTO FUCKING SWANS. HONK HONK MOTHERFUCKER.

LIR EVENTUALLY FINDS OUT ABOUT HIS KIDS AND TRIES TO MAKE THEM NORMAL AGAIN. HE CAN'T BECAUSE AOIFE HAD FUCKING CURSED THEM FOR 900 YEARS.

900 YEARS LATER THE SWAN KIDS ARE STILL HAVING A SHITTY TIME BEING SWANS. EVENTUALLY THEY STUMBLE UPON A MONK, WHO SOMEHOW WORKS OUT WHAT FUCKERY HAS OCCURED, USING HIS MONK POWERS, TURNS THEM HUMAN AGAIN AND CONVERTS THEM TO CHRISTIANITY. OH BUT SINCE THEY WERE 900 YEARS OLD THEY AGED SUPER QUICK AND WERE SOON DEAD. WHAT A LOVELY STORY.

DEATH RAY GIANTS

BALOR IS A FOMORIAN (FUCKING ANGRY IRISH GIANTS). EVERYONE IS FUCKING TERRIFIED OF HIM, BECAUSE HE'S FUCKING MASSIVE AND CAN SHOOT DEATH RAYS OUT OF HIS SINGLE EYE. HE STOMPS AROUND THE PLACE FUCKING SHIT UP AND LASERING ENTIRE ARMIES TO DEATH, UNTIL ONE DAY HE HEARS A PROPHECY THAT HIS GRANDSON WILL KILL HIM. BALOR DOESN'T HAVE A GRANDSON YET, SO HE LOCKS HIS ONLY DAUGHTER IN A TOWER SO SHE NEVER BECOMES PREGNANT. WHAT A DICK.

UNFORTUNATELY, BALOR HAS MADE A BUNCH OF ENEMIES. ONE OF THESE IS A DUDE CALLED MAC CINNFHAELAIDH, WHO'S PRETTY FUCKING PISSED OFF BECAUSE BALOR STOLE HIS FAVOURITE COW. MAC CINNFHAELAIDH VOWS REVENGE AGAINST BALOR (HE REALLY FUCKING LOVED THAT COW) AND SNEAKS INTO THE TOWER, WHERE HE SPITEFULLY FUCKS BALOR'S DAUGHTER JUST AS A FORM OF FUCKED-UP REVENGE.

BALOR'S DAUGHTER GIVES BIRTH TO TRIPLETS, SO HE PUTS THEM IN A BAG AND THROWS THEM IN THE FUCKING SEA. HE SHOULD HAVE JUST JUMPED ON THEM OR SOMETHING, BECAUSE ONE OF THEM SURVIVES AND GROWS UP TO SHOOT HIM IN THE FACE TILL HE DIES. AND THAT'S WHY IF YOU'RE GOING TO KILL A BABY YOU SHOULD DO IT FUCKING PROPERLY, WITH NONE OF THIS ABANDONING-IN-THE-WILDERNESS BULLSHIT. GET IT FUCKING RIGHT.

EXPLODING BRAIN DEATH

CONCHOBHAR IS A FUCKING DICK. HIS MOTHER PROMISES TO MARRY KING FERGUS OF ULSTER IF HE LETS CONCHOBHAR BE KING FOR A YEAR, BUT CONCHOBHAR DOESN'T PLAY BY THE RULES AND JUST KEEPS THE THRONE. WHAT A FUCKING SHITBAG.

CONCHOBHAR SPENDS MANY YEARS BEING A SHIT KING AND GENERALLY A DICKWEASEL. HE KILLS PEASANTS AND BEATS WOMEN AND FALLS IN LOVE WITH HIS OWN ADOPTED DAUGHTER. EVERYTHING IS SHIT FOR EVERYONE IN THE AREA, AND EVENTUALLY SEVERAL PEOPLE DECIDE THEY'VE HAD ENOUGH OF HIS SHIT.

CONALL HAS SPENT A FEW MONTHS BEATING THE SHIT OUT OF OTHER KINGS, AND EVENTUALLY HE DECIDES TO GO FOR CONCHOBHAR. HE MAKES A BALL OUT OF MUD AND THE BRAIN OF HIS LAST VICTIM, AND SETS OUT TO MURDER CONCHOBHAR WITH IT.

THERE'S A FUCKING MASSIVE BATTLE, WHICH CONCHOBHAR WINS. IT'S A FUCKING DISASTER AND HE STAYS KING, BECAUSE THE REVOLUTIONARIES WERE ALL FUCKING SHIT. HOWEVER, CONALL HITS HIM IN THE HEAD WITH THE BRAIN BALL AND IT LODGES IN THE MIDDLE OF HIS BRAIN. SEVEN YEARS LATER, AFTER YEARS OF BEING A SHIT KING, HE GETS REALLY FUCKING ANGRY AND SHOUTS A LITTLE BIT TOO LOUDLY, AND THE BALL OF BRAIN STUCK IN HIS BRAIN EXPLODES AND SPLITS HIS ENTIRE MOTHERFUCKING HEAD IN HALF, WHICH (UNSURPRISINGLY) KILLS HIM. IT'S A BIT LATE BUT AT LEAST HE'S FUCKING DEAD.

FUCKING UP THE WEDDING

DECHTIRE IS THE DAUGHTER OF THE FUCKING LOVE GOD AONGHUS AND THE DRUID CATHBAD. SHE'S IN THE MIDDLE OF HER WEDDING TO SUALTAM, THE CHIEFTAIN OF ULSTER, WHEN THE GOD LUGH TURNS INTO A MOTHERFUCKING MAYFLY AND FALLS INTO HER DRINK. WHEN SHE DRINKS HIM, LUGH PUTS HER IN A MAGICAL SLEEP, RUINING THE WEDDING COMPLETELY. WHAT A FUCKING DICK.

WHILE DECHTIRE IS ASLEEP, LUGH COMES TO HER IN A DREAM AND TELLS HER TO RUN AWAY WITH HIM AND TAKE FIFTY HOT GIRLS WITH HER. WHEN SHE WAKES UP, SHE ROUNDS UP FIFTY OF HER HOTTEST FRIENDS AND LUGH TURNS THEM ALL INTO FUCKING BIRDS AND THEY ALL FUCK OFF TOGETHER, LEAVING SUALTAM REALLY FUCKING CONFUSED.

NINE MONTHS LATER, DECHTIRE GIVES BIRTH TO A BABY. FUCKING SUSPICIOUS. THEN SHE COMES HOME AND DECLARES THAT SUALTAM IS THE FATHER (HE PROBABLY ISN'T. SHE'S A FUCKING LIAR) AND THAT THE BABY IS CALLED SETANTA. LATER, THOUGH, HE GROWS UP TO BE THE FUCKING MAJESTIC HERO CU CHULAINN.

BRUTAL PUPPY MURDER

WHEN SETANTA IS ONLY A MOTHERFUCKING SIX YEAR OLD, HE'S ALREADY SUPER STRONG. KING CONCHOBHAR (WHO, AS PREVIOUSLY ESTABLISHED, IS A FUCKING DICKWEASEL) INVITES HIM TO A PARTY IN ORDER TO INSPECT THE KID. THERE, HE SETS THE FUCKING MASSIVE ANGRY MURDER DOG OF CULANN THE SMITH ON SETANTA, JUST TO SEE WHAT HAPPENS. CONCHOBHAR IS A FUCKING AWFUL PERSON.

SETANTA STICKS HIS FAVOURITE BALL IN THE DOG'S MOUTH AND SMASHES ITS HEAD INTO A ROCK, MURDERING IT AND SPLATTERING DOGGY BRAINS ALL OVER THE MOTHERFUCKING FLOOR. SETANTA IS A HEARTLESS LITTLE SHIT WHO DOESN'T LIKE DOGS.

CULANN IS FUCKING FURIOUS THAT SETANTA HAS MURDERED HIS FAVOURITE PUPPY, AND DEMANDS A REPLACEMENT. BEING A SEVEN YEAR OLD AND THEREFORE FUCKING RIDICULOUS, SETANTA PROMISES TO BE A REPLACEMENT DOG TILL HE CAN FIND A SUITABLE PUPPY TO GIVE CULANN. HE CHANGES HIS NAME TO CU CHULAINN (THE HOUND OF CULANN), AND SETS OUT ON A LIFE OF HEROICS AND FUCKING SHIT UP.

OH SHIT, A PROPHECY

ONE DAY, WHEN HE'S STILL ABOUT SEVEN FUCKING YEARS OLD, CU CHULAINN OVERHEARS A PROPHECY FROM CATHBAD THE DRUID. THE PROPHECY SAYS THAT ANY WARRIOR WHO GETS A NEW SWORD THAT DAY WILL BE REALY FUCKING GREAT AND FAMOUS. CU CHULAINN GETS WAY TOO FUCKING EXCITED BY THIS AND GOES TO ASK CONCHOBHAR FOR A SWORD, BECAUSE HE'S A FUCKING MENACE OF A SEVEN YEAR OLD.

CONCHOBHAR THINKS THIS IDEA IS FUCKING GREAT, AND GIVES CU CHULAINN A SWORD. HE BREAKS IT. THE LITTLE SHIT IS JUST THAT FUCKING STRONG. THIS HAPPENS SEVERAL TIMES, AND IN THE END CONCHOBHAR JUST GIVES HIM HIS OWN MAGICAL SWORD, BECAUSE GIVING MURDEROUS SEVEN YEAR OLDS MAGIC WEAPONS IS A FUCKING GREAT IDEA.

NOW CU CHULAINN IS ARMED AND HAPPY, BUT ALL IS NOT WELL. HE'S A FUCKING IDIOT, AND FORGOT TO LISTEN TO THE SECOND HALF OF THE MOTHERFUCKING PROPHECY. YES, HE'S GOING TO BE FAMOUS AND SHIT LIKE THAT, BUT HE'S ALSO GOING TO DIE REALLY FUCKING YOUNG. HE'S COMPLETELY OBLIVIOUS, THOUGH, AND FUCKS OFF TO STAB THE SHIT OUT OF ANYONE HE DOESN'T LIKE THE LOOK OF.

CHILDREN ARE FUCKING TERRIFYING

THE THREE SHITTY SONS OF SOME DUDE CALLED NECHTAN SCENE ARE HANGING AROUND BOASTING THAT THEY'VE KILLED MORE THAN HALF THE FUCKING POPULATION OF ULSTER AND GENERALLY BEING DICKBAGS. WHEN HE HEARS ABOUT IT, CU CHULAINN IS FUCKING FURIOUS, SO HE GOES TO GET HIS FAVOURITE SPEAR AND MANGLE THE SHIT OUT OF THEM. HE'S ONLY ABOUT NINE YEARS OLD, BUT THAT WON'T STOP HIM FROM STABBING A BITCH OR THREE.

WHEN HE GETS TO THEM, CU CHULAINN GOES INTO AN UNCONTROLLABLE FUCKING INSANE RAGE OF STABBINESS AND DEATH, AND KILLS ALL THREE OF THEM WITHOUT TAKING A SCRATCH. THERE'S BLOOD EVERYWHERE AND GUTS HANGING IN THE TREES AND ALL THE LOCAL WILDLIFE HAS BEEN SEVERELY TRAUMATISED, BUT CU CHULAINN IS FINE. HE'S ONE HELL OF A FUCKING SCARY NINE YEAR OLD. HE'S STILL CRAZY AND STABBY, BUT HE FUCKS OFF HOME ANYWAY.

WHEN HE GETS HOME, EVERYONE IN THE VILLAGE PANICS BECAUSE HE'S STILL ON A FUCKING RAMPAGE AND MIGHT KILL THEM ALL. IN A HEROIC ATTEMPT TO DISTRACT HIM, ALL THE WOMEN IN THE VILLAGE TAKE THEIR TOPS OFF AND STAND IN FRONT OF HIM, BUT IT DOESN'T WORK. CU CHULAINN IS NINE FUCKING YEARS OLD. HE DOESN'T GIVE A SHIT ABOUT BOOBS.

IN THE END THEY DECIDE TO DROP HIM IN COLD WATER TO MAKE HIM CALM THE FUCK DOWN. THEY GRAB HIM BY THE ANKLES AND DUMP HIM IN A BARREL OF WATER, BUT HE'S SO ANGRY IT JUST FUCKING EXPLODES. THEN THEY PUT HIM IN ANOTHER BARREL OF WATER, AND HE'S STILL REALLY FUCKING ANGRY BUT NOT QUITE AS BAD AS HE WAS, SO THIS ONE JUST BOILS. THEN THEY PUT HIM IN A THIRD BARREL OF WATER, AND THIS ONE JUST HEATS UP TO A FUCKING PERFECT TEMPERATURE. AFTER THAT THEY PRESUMABLY FETCH HIM HIS RUBBER DUCKY AND LET HIM CALM THE FUCK DOWN IN HIS NICE WARM BATH.

[OBLIGATORY TRAINING MONTAGE]

WHEN HE'S A YOUNG MAN, CU CHULAINN IS SO FUCKING HOT THAT ALL THE MEN OF ULSTER ARE FUCKING TERRIFIED THAT HE'S GOING TO STEAL THEIR WIVES AND FUCK THEIR DAUGHTERS. THEY'RE ALL INSECURE FUCKS, AND THEY SHOULDN'T WORRY AT ALL. CU CHULAINN DOESN'T GIVE A FUCK ABOUT ANY WOMEN EXCEPT EMER, THE DAUGHTER OF FORGALL, WHO IS A FUCKING DICK.

FORGALL REALLY FUCKING HATES CU CHULAINN, SO HE SUGGESTS THAT HE FUCKS OFF FOR HERO TRAINING WITH SCATHACH, THE CRAZY SCOTTISH WARRIOR WOMAN, HOPING THAT HE HAS A TRAGIC ACCIDENT AND FUCKING DIES IN THE PROCESS.

THAT DOESN'T HAPPEN THOUGH, BECAUSE CU CHULAINN IS AS MUCH OF A CRAZY MOTHERFUCKER AS SCATHACH. HE LEARNS TO DO ALL SORTS OF CRAZY HEROIC SHIT LIKE THROWING SPEARS WITH HIS FEET.

EVENTUALLY, THOUGH, HIS HAPPY TRAINING MONTAGE IS INTERRUPTED BY SCATHACH'S EVIL TWIN SISTER, AIFE, ATTACKING THE TRAINING CAMP. CU CHULAINN AND AIFE ARE EVENLY MATCHED, BUT HE'S A DEVIOUS LITTLE SHIT, AND TELLS HER HER FAVOURITE HORSE AND CHARIOT ARE FALLING OFF A MOTHERFUCKING CLIFF BEHIND HER. WHEN SHE TURNS AROUND TO LOOK, HE STABS HER A FEW TIMES AND DECLARES HIMSELF THE WINNER. SHE DOESN'T DIE THOUGH, SO HE MAKES HER PROMISE TO STOP TRYING TO FUCK SHIT UP FOR SCATHACH. THEN THEY FUCK AND HE LEAVES.

WHEN HE RETURNS TO IRELAND, CU CHULAINN KIDNAPS EMER, STEALS ALL OF FORGALL'S TREASURE AND PUSHES FORGALL OUT OF A WINDOW TO HIS DEATH. CU CHULAINN IS A BIG FAN OF WINDOW PAIN. HE'S ALSO A DICK, BUT THAT WAS PRETTY FUCKING OBVIOUS.

CU CHULAINN FUCKS UP

CU CHULAINN HAS A SON. REMEMBER THAT TIME HE TRICKED A CRAZY SCOTTISH WARRIOR QUEEN INTO THINKING HER HORSE FELL OFF A CLIFF AND THEN FUCKED HER? WELL, SHE HAD A KID, AND IT'S HIS.

CU CHULAINN ASKS CONNLA (HIS SON) TO COME AND VISIT HIM, BUT MAKES HIM PROMISE THREE REALLY FUCKING STUPID THINGS: TO NOT TURN BACK ONCE HE'S STARTED HIS JOURNEY, TO NOT REFUSE A CHALLENGE ON THE WAY, AND TO NOT TELL ANYONE HIS NAME. THERE ISN'T A REASON FOR ANY OF THESE, CU CHULAINN IS JUST A SHIT DAD.

CONNLA SETS OFF ON HIS JOURNEY, MERRILY SLAUGHTERING ANYONE HE ENCOUNTERS, AND EVENTUALLY HE MAKES IT TO CU CHULAINN'S HOUSE.

CU CHULAINN OPENS THE DOOR AND ASKS CONNLA WHAT HIS FUCKING NAME IS, AND CONNLA REFUSES, BECAUSE HE'S PROMISED. CU CHULAINN IS PRETTY FUCKING ANNOYED, AND CHALLENGES CONNLA TO A DUEL. THEY HAVE A FUCKING MASSIVE FIGHT, AND CONNLA FIGHTS SO WELL THAT CU CHULLAIN GOES INTO ANOTHER UNCONTROLLABLE ANGRY FUCKING STABBY RAGE. CONNLA GETS STABBED TO DEATH, AND AS HE LIES THERE DYING HE FINALLY SAYS HIS NAME.

CU CHULANN REALISES THAT HE'S JUST MURDERED HIS OWN FUCKING SON FOR NO GOOD REASON, AND BREAKS DOWN IN TEARS. HE'S A SHIT DAD AND HE'S FUCKED UP, AND EVERYTHING IS HIS FAULT. WHAT A FUCKING IDIOT.

CU CHULAINN ADOPTS A WEIRD MUTANT INCEST BABY

THERE'S A FUCKING MASSIVE BATTLE ABOUT TO HAPPEN, AND THE THREE CRAZY FUCKING WARRIOR TRIPLETS, BRES, NAR AND LOTHAR, ARE PREPARING TO FIGHT THEIR OWN FATHER. THE NIGHT BEFORE THE BATTLE, THOUGH, THEIR SISTER CLOTHRU STARTS TO FREAK THE FUCK OUT ABOUT HOW THEY MIGHT ALL DIE WITHOUT HEIRS, AND DECIDES TO FIX THAT.

SHE SNEAKS INTO ALL THREE OF THEIR BEDS AND FUCKS ALL OF THEM. IT'S FUCKED UP AND INCESTUOUS, BUT SHE DOESN'T GIVE A FUCK. NINE MONTHS LATER, SHE HAS A SON.

HIS NAME IS LUGAID RIAB NDERG (LUGAID THE RED STRIPED), BECAUSE HE HAS MOTHERFUCKING RED STRIPES DIVIDING HIM NEATLY INTO THREE. LUGAID LOOKS EXACTLY LIKE HIS DAD. IN FACT, HE LOOKS EXACTLY LIKE ALL THREE OF HIS FUCKING DADS. HIS HEAD LOOKS LIKE NAR, HIS CHEST AND ARMS LOOK LIKE BRES, AND HIIS LEGS LOOK LIKE LOTHAR. HE'S PRETTY FUCKING WEIRD, AND THAT'S WHY YOU SHOULDN'T HAVE INCEST BABIES WITH THREE DADS.

CU CHULAINN ADOPTS LUGAID, AND DECLARES THAT HE SHOULD BE HIGH KING. HE PLOPS THE KID ON THE CORONATION STONE, WHICH IS MEANT TO SHOUT WHEN THAT HAPPENS, AND NOTHING FUCKING HAPPENS, SO HE GETS REALLY FUCKING ANGRY AND CUTS THE STONE IN HALF TO TEACH IT A MOTHERFUCKING LESSON. LUGAID BECOMES HIGH KING ANYWAY, BECAUSE NOBODY REALLY GIVES A FUCK ABOUT TALKING ROCKS.

LITERAL PISSING CONTEST

ON ONE OF HIS BULLSHIT ADVENTURES, CU CHULAINN SAVES THE LIFE OF A SCANDINAVIAN PRINCESS CALLED DERBFORGAILL. SOME TIME LATER, SHE REALISES THAT SHE'S FALLEN MADLY IN LOVE WITH HIM, SO SHE TURNS INTO A SWAN AND FUCKS OFF TO IRELAND TO VISIT HIM.

UNFORTUNATELY, CU CHULAINN REALLY FUCKING HATES SWANS, SO HE SHOOTS HER WITH A SLING. SHE TURNS BACK INTO A PERSON, AND HE REALISES THAT HE'S FUCKED UP, SO HE SUCKS THE FUCKING STONE OUT OF THE WOUND. UNFORTUNATELY FOR HER, BECAUSE HE'S TASTED HER BLOOD HE CAN'T MARRY HER (ALSO HE ALREADY HAS A WIFE, BUT SHE DOESN'T GIVE A FUCK ABOUT THAT). INSTEAD, HE MARRIES HER OFF TO HIS WEIRD ADOPTED MUTANT INCEST SON LUGAID.

IN THE WINTER, THE WOMEN OF THE TOWN HAVE A LITERAL PISSING CONTEST TO SEE WHO CAN PISS DEEPEST INTO THE SNOW AND THUS PROVE HERSELF THE MOST DESIRABLE. ULSTER HAS PRETTY FUCKING WEIRD STANDARDS OF BEAUTY. DERBFORGAILL WINS, AND ALL THE OTHER WOMEN ARE SO JEALOUS THAT THEY CUT OFF HER NOSE AND EARS AND HAIR AND PULL OUT HER FUCKING EYES. THEY'RE REALLY FUCKING JEALOUS, OK. SHE DIES OF HER INJURIES, AND WHEN LUGAID FINDS OUT HE DIES OF GRIEF. IT'S ALL FUCKING TRAGIC, BUT THEN CU CHULAINN FUCKS IT ALL UP EVEN MORE.

IN THE MIDDLE OF THE NIGHT, HE SETS FIRE TO THE HOUSE WHERE ALL THE WOMEN SLEEP, AND ALL 150 OF THEM BURN TO FUCKING DEATH. NOW EVERYONE IS FUCKING DEAD AND NOBODY IS HAPPY. IT'S A FUCKING TRAGEDY.

COW FIGHT!

ULSTER IS UNDER ATTACK BY MEDB, THE QUEEN OF CONNACHT. MEDB WANTS TO STEAL THE TOWN'S MAGIC FUCKING COW (IT USED TO BE A PERSON, NOW IT'S A MAGIC COW. JUST ACCEPT IT. IRELAND IS FUCKING WEIRD SOMETIMES). SHE STRIKES ALL THE MEN OF ULSTER EXCEPT CU CHULAINN DOWN WITH SOME BULLSHIT MAGIC PLAGUE, AND SENDS IN THE ARMY.

CU CHULAINN IS MEANT TO BE GUARDING THE BORDER, BUT HE'S AT HOME FUCKING HIS WIFE INSTEAD SO THE ARMY JUST WALK STRAIGHT IN. FORTUNATELY, HE MANAGES TO GET IN THE WAY BEFORE THEY MAKE IT ACROSS THE FUCKING RIVER. ON THE WAY, THOUGH, HE RUNS INTO A REALLY HOT HALF-NAKED GIRL, WHO OFFERS HIM SEX. HE TELLS HER TO FUCK OFF, BECAUSE HE'S GOT SHIT TO DO. AT THIS POINT SHE REVEALS HERSELF TO BE THE MORRIGAN (SUPER IMPORTANT WITCHY GODDESS) AND TELLS HIM HE'S FUCKED UP, BUT HE DOESN'T GIVE A SHIT.

WHEN HE GETS TO THE RIVER, HE CHALLENGES EVERY MAN IN THE ARMY TO SINGLE COMBAT AS THEY CROSS THE FORD, AND SPENDS SEVERAL MONTHS BEATING THE SHIT OUT OF THEM ONE AT A TIME. THE MORRIGAN IS DETERMINED TO FUCK SHIT UP FOR HIM, THOUGH, SO SHE TURNS INTO AN EEL AND ATTACKS HIM. HE BREAKS HALF HER FUCKING RIBS. THEN SHE TURNS INTO A WOLF AND HE POKES HER EYE OUT. THEN SHE TURNS INTO A COW AND HE BREAKS HER FUCKING LEGS. THEN SHE JUST FUCKS OFF AND LEAVES HIM ALONE.

AFTER A WHILE, CU CHULAINN GETS SO ANGRY THAT HE GOES INTO ANOTHER UNCONTROLLABLE STABBY MURDER RAGE, AND SLAUGHTERS EVERY SINGLE MAN IN THE ARMY SINGLE HANDEDLY. HE'S ONE HELL OF A MURDEROUS MOTHERFUCKER. THEN HE BUILDS NEW FORTIFICATIONS FOR THE TOWN. OUT OF MOTHERFUCKING MANGLED DEAD BODIES. WHAT THE FUCK. THERE'S BLOOD EVERYWHERE, AND HE DOESN'T GIVE A SHIT. HE JUST SITS THERE HAPPILY BUILDING WALLS. CU CHULAINN IS A FUCKING LUNATIC.

THE DEATH OF CU CHULAINN

WHAT, YOU THOUGHT HE MIGHT HAVE A HAPPY ENDING? FUCK OFF. IT'S IMPOSSIBLE TO AVOID A PROPHECY.

MEDB, THE QUEEN WHO REALLY WANTED THAT MAGIC COW, TEAMS UP WITH LUGALD AND VARIOUS OTHER PEOPLE WITH A GRUDGE AGAINST CU CHULAINN (THERE ARE A SHITLOAD OF THOSE. CU CHULAINN IS KIND OF A DICK) AND THEY SET OUT TO BEAT THE SHIT OUT OF HIM.

LUGALD MAKES THREE FUCKING MAGIC SPEARS, AND DECLARES THAT EACH ONE WILL KILL A KING. THEN THE FUCKING MASSIVE FINAL BATTLE STARTS. HE MURDERS CU CHULAINN'S CHARIOTEER (THE KING OF CHARIOTEERS) WITH THE FIRST, THEN HE MURDERS CU CHULAINN'S HORSE (THE KING OF HORSES) WITH THE SECOND, AND FINALLY HE STABS CU CHULAINN IN THE STOMACH WITH THE THIRD. CU CHULAINN ISN'T DEAD YET, BUT HE'S DYING.

HE SLAUGHTERS HIS WAY THROUGH HALF OF MEDB'S ARMY ALL ON HIS FUCKING OWN, BUT IN THE END HE'S TOO WEAK TO STAND. WHAT DOES HE DO? HE PULLS OUT HIS OWN MOTHERFUCKING INTESTINES THOUGH THE HOLE IN HIS SIDE, AND TIES HIMSELF TO A STANDING STONE WITH THEM SO HE DOESN'T FALL OVER. NEATLY TIED TO A ROCK WITH HIS OWN INTESTINES IN A PRETTY FUCKING BOW, HE SLAUGHTERS HIS WAY THROUGH MOST OF THE REST OF THE ARMY. CU CHULAINN IS A FUCKING MENACE.

IN THE END HE DIES FROM LOSS OF INTERNAL ORGANS (THEY'RE TIED ROUND A FUCKING STONE, THERE'S NO FUCKING WAY HE COULD SURVIVE SHIT LIKE THAT), AND LUGALD CUTS OFF HIS HEAD. THE SWORD FALLS FROM CU CHULAINNS DEAD LIFELESS FUCKING HANDS AND LANDS ON LUGALD'S WRIST, CUTTING HIS HAND OFF. EVEN DEAD AND HEADLESS, CU CHULAINN IS FUCKING DANGEROUS.

CU CHULAINN'S FRIEND CONALL HAS SWORN TO AVENGE HIM, THOUGH, SO HE CHALLENGES LUGALD TO A DUEL. IN ORDER TO MAKE THINGS FAIR, HE STICKS ONE HAND IN HIS POCKET FOR

THE FIGHT. IN THE END HIS HORSE JUST BITES LUGALD TO DEATH THOUGH.

PRETTY MUCH EVERYONE IS FUCKING DEAD, THERE'S BLOOD EVERYWHERE, AND EVERYTHING IS SHIT. IT'S ABOUT TO GET WORSE, THOUGH, BECAUSE WHEN EVERYONE'S WIVES/SISTERS/DAUGHTERS FIND OUT ABOUT THE FUCKING CARNAGE, THEY ALL DIE OF FUCKING GRIEF. NOW EVERYONE IS FUCKING DEAD. NO HAPPY ENDINGS HERE, BITCHES.

CHINESE MYTHOLOGY

BEGINNINGS: CHINESE STYLE

AT THE BEGINNING OF TIME, ALL THERE IS IN THE UNIVERSE IS A FUCKING EGG. IT'S A FUCKING MASSIVE EGG, BUT IT'S STILL AN EGG. IN THE MIDDLE OF THE EGG IS THE FIRST GOD, PAN GU. PAN GU IS A FUCKING GIANT, BUT HE LIKES TO NAP. HE SLEEPS FOR THOUSANDS OF YEARS, BUT EVENTUALLY HE DECIDES HE'S HAD ENOUGH OF THIS SHIT AND STANDS UP, PUSHING THE TOP OF THE FUCKING EGG OFF. THE TOP OF THE EGG MAKES THE SKY, AND THE BOTTOM IS THE EARTH.

PAN GU IS WORRIED THAT THE EARTH AND SKY MIGHT STICK TOGETHER AGAIN AND LEAVE HIM WITH JUST A MOTHERFUCKING EGG FOR COMPANY, SO HE SLIPS INTO THE GAP AND PUSHES THE SKY UP.

HE STAYS THERE, STANDING STILL AND PUSHING THE SKY UP, FOR A WHOLE EIGHTEEN THOUSAND FUCKING YEARS. THAT'S ONE FUCKING HELL OF A LONG TIME, EVEN FOR A GOD. EVERY DAY HE PUSHES UP A BIT MORE, AND EVERY DAY HE GROWS A TINY BIT TALLER.

AFTER EIGHTEEN THOUSAND YEARS HE'S THIRTY THOUSAND MOTHERFUCKING MILES TALL, WHICH IS JUST FUCKING INSANE. THEN HE HAS A NAP. AGAIN.

THIS TIME, THOUGH, BECAUSE HE'S BEEN STANDING THERE FOR EIGHTEEN THOUSAND FUCKING YEARS, HE DIES IN HIS SLEEP. HE'S FUCKING ANCIENT, EVEN GODS DIE SOMETIMES. HIS HEAD TURNS INTO MOUNTAINS, HIS BLOOD BECOMES WATER, HIS BEARD BECOMES FLOWERS. IT'S ALL REALLY FUCKING POETIC, BUT NOW GOD IS DEAD AND THAT'S PRETTY FUCKED UP.

WHERE DO (CHINESE) PEOPLE COME FROM?

AFTER THE WORLD HAS BEEN CREATED, EVERYTHING IS RULED BY THE CHIEF GODDESS NU WA. NU WA IS ONE FUCKING WEIRD GODDESS. SHE'S A FUCKING HUGE SNAKE WITH A HUMAN HEAD, AND SHE CAN FUCKING SHAPESHIFT. SHE STILL STAYS IN HER MOTHERFUCKING SNAKE LADY SHAPE MOST OF THE TIME, EVEN THOUGH IT'S REALLY FUCKING IMPRACTICAL.

NU WA THINKS THE WORLD IS TOO QUIET AND BORING, SO SHE DECIDES TO MAKE PEOPLE. SHE SITS DOWN BY THE RIVER, GROWS A PAIR OF HANDS, AND STARTS SCULPTING THE FUCKING CLAY. SHE DECIDES NOT TO MAKE PEOPLE THAT LOOK LIKE HER, BECAUSE EVEN SHE ACCEPTS THAT THE SNAKE BODY IS FUCKING SILLY.

SHE MAKES A BUNCH OF LITTLE CLAY DUDES AND BRINGS THEM TO LIFE, AND THEN SHE GETS BORED AND STARTS SPLASHING MUD EVERYWHERE, WHICH MAKES SHITTY PEOPLE BUT SHE BRINGS THEM TO LIFE TOO.

THEN SHE DECLARES THAT ALL THE FUCKING CLAY PEOPLE SHOULD BE RICH AND FORTUNATE, AND THE MUD PEOPLE SHOULD BE POOR AND MISERABLE AND GENERALLY HAVE SHIT LIVES. AND THAT'S HOW MOTHERFUCKING CLASS DIVISIONS BEGIN. IT ALL TURNS OUT FINE IN THE END, BUT IT WAS A SHITTY APPROACH TO MAKING PEOPLE.

THE SKY IS FALLING

ONE DAY, A FUCKING HUGE CHUNK OF SKY FALLS DOWN. THIS IS A FUCKING DISASTER, BECAUSE IT MAKES A MASSIVE DENT IN THE EARTH, CRUSHES SEVERAL PEOPLE, AND LEAVES A FUCKING MASSIVE HOLE IN THE SKY. NU WA IS FUCKING MISERABLE ABOUT THIS SHIT, SO SHE SETS OUT TO FIX IT.

SHE MAKES A SHIT-TONNE OF FUCKING MAGIC SUPERGLUE, AND GLUES THE MISSING BIT OF SKY BACK IN PLACE. SHE'S NOT SURE THAT'S ENOUGH, THOUGH, SO SHE DECIDES TO PROP IT UP AND REINFORCE IT.

SHE CAPTURES ONE OF THE GIANT IMMORTAL TURTLES THAT HANG OUT AT THE BOTTOM OF THE SEA, AND CUTS ITS FUCKING LEGS OFF. THE POOR TURTLE, BEING FUCKING IMMORTAL, DOESN'T DIE. IT JUST LIES THERE WITH NO LEGS LOOKING SAD BECAUSE EVERYTHING IS A BIT SHIT FOR IT NOW. NU WA TAKES THE GIANT TURTLE LEGS, AND USES THOSE TO PROP UP THE SKY.

THE WORLD IS SAFE FROM BEING CRUSHED BY LUMPS OF SKY, BUT ALL THE EFFORT OF FIXING THIS SHIT IS TOO MUCH FOR NU WA, AND SHE FUCKING DIES. IT'S OK, THOUGH, BECAUSE HER BODY TURNS INTO A THOUSAND MOTHERFUCKING FAIRIES WHO HANG AROUND AND WATCH OVER THE HUMAN RACE FOR EVER.

MERCILESS DRAGON MURDER

LADY YIN IS PREGNANT. SHE'S BEEN PREGNANT FOR THREE AND A HALF FUCKING YEARS. EVEN BY MYTHOLOGICAL STANDARDS, THAT'S PRETTY FUCKING WEIRD.

ONE DAY SHE GIVES BIRTH. CONGRATU-FUCKING-LATIONS, IT'S....A GIANT BALL OF FLESH. GROSS. OUT OF THE FLESH-BALL CRAWLS NEZHA, A CUTE LIL TODDLER WHO WILL GO ON TO BE THE HERO OF OUR TALE.

ONE TIME SOME LOCAL FUCKERS WANT RAIN, BECAUSE EVERYTHING HAS BEEN DRY AND GENERALLY SHIT. SO THEY SACRIFICE SOME LOVELY FOOD TO AO KUANG, THE MOTHERFUCKING EAST SEA DRAGON KING. AO KUANG WON'T TAKE ANY OF THIS SHIT BECAUSE HE WANTS TO EAT SOME FUCKING CHILDREN, NOT THIS SHITTY FOOD.

HE SENDS A MINION TO CATCH HIM SOME KIDDIES. THE KIDDIES HAPPEN TO BE NEZHA'S FRIENDS. OH HELL NO. NEZHA BEATS THE SHIT OUT OF THE MINION AND HE COMES LIMPING HOME TO AO KUANG, WHO SENDS OUT SOMEONE MORE BADASS, HIS OWN SON AO BING.

BUT NEZHA KILLS AO BING BECAUSE HE'S A FUCKING BADASS CHILD. AO KUANG GETS SUPER PISSED AND CALLS UP HIS DRAGON HOMIES, AND THEY THREATEN TO FLOOD NEZHA'S HOME.

SO NEZHA COMMITS SUICIDE TO APPEASE THE DRAGONS, CUTTING HIMSELF TO PIECES TO BE LIKE THE FLESH-BALL HE WAS BORN FROM. WHAT THE ACTUAL FUCK.

LATER HIS MAMA BUILDS HIM A FUCKING TEMPLE BECAUSE TEMPLES ARE FUCKING GREAT. THEN NEZHA'S FATHER BURNS IT DOWN BECAUSE HE'S A LITTLE BITCH. EVENTUALLY NEZHA GETS REBORN AND EVERYTHING'S FUCKING GREAT.

FUCKED-UP VAMPIRE DRAGONS

IN CHINA, THERE ARE DRAGONS. FUCKLOADS OF DRAGONS. SOME OF THEM ARE NICE DRAGONS, BUT SOME OF THEM ARE JUST FUCKING HORRIFIC.

ONE DAY, SOME GUY GOES FOR A WALK IN THE COUNTRYSIDE. GOOD IDEA? FUCK NO.

HE WALKS DOWN TO THE RIVERBANK AND WANDERS ALONG THE RIVERSIDE. UNFORTUNATELY, THE RIVER IS FULL OF MOTHERFUCKING DRAGONS, AND ONE OF THEM HAPPENS TO EAT PEOPLE. THE DRAGON IN QUESTION IS HALF SNAKE, HALF TIGER, AND ALL HUNGRY. ALSO IT QUACKS LIKE A DUCK. WHAT THE FUCK.

IT JUMPS OUT OF THE WATER AND SPITS ALL OVER THE POOR HARMLESS GUY. HE'S COVERED IN DRAGON SPIT, WHICH IS FUCKING REVOLTING, AND STOPS HIM FROM MOVING. WHILE HE'S TRAPPED LIKE THIS, THE DRAGON SNEAKS UP ON HIM, STICKS ITS FACE IN HIS ARMPIT AND DRINKS HIS BLOOD.

VAMPIRE DRAGONS AREN'T NICE AND HARMLESS. IT DRINKS ALL HIS BLOOD, AND WHEN HIS FAMILY WONDER WHAT'S HAPPENED TO HIM AND GO LOOKING, THEY FIND HIM LYING ON THE FLOOR, COMPLETELY DRAINED OF BLOOD. IT'S MISERABLE AND HORRIBLE, AND NOBODY GETS A HAPPY ENDING. EXCEPT THE DRAGON.

HOW MANY EMPERORS HAVE YOU SEEN TODAY?

THE CELESTIAL FATHER IS HAVING A BABY. FUCK YES. IT'S A 25 MONTH PREGNANCY, BECAUSE GODS DON'T GIVE A FUCK ABOUT HUMAN NORMS. AS SOON AS HE'S BORN, BABY HUANG TI CAN SPEAK IN EVERY LANGUAGE. ALSO HE HAS FOUR FUCKING HEADS, BUT THAT'S NO BIG FUCKING DEAL.

BY THE TIME HE'S AN ADULT, HUANG TI HAS MADE FRIENDS WITH EVERY SINGLE FUCKING MAGIC BIRD IN THE ENTIRE FUCKING WORLD. HIS HOUSE IS COVERED IN FUCKING PHOENIXES AND SPACE OWLS AND CRAZY SHIT LIKE THAT.

THE FIVE MOST POWERFUL GODS DECIDE TO FUCK OFF DOWN TO EARTH, BUT NONE OF THEM HAVE A FUCKING CLUE WHO SHOULD BE THE EMPEROR. THEY SETTLE THIS IN THE MOST SENSIBLE WAY, WITH A MOTHERFUCKING BATTLE. IN THE END HUANG TI WINS, AND DECLARES HIMSELF THE YELLOW EMPEROR, BUT THE OTHER FOUR ALL FUCK OFF TO DIFFERENT PARTS OF THE WORLD, DECLARE THEMSELVES EMPERORS IN THEIR OWN PLACES, AND PLOT THEIR FUCKING RETURN. THERE'S A WHOLE MOTHERFUCKING RAINBOW OF EMPERORS.

HUANG TI MAKES A FUCKING MASSIVE PALACE ON TOP OF A MOUNTAIN. IT'S MADE OF FUCKING JADE AND SURROUNDED BY MOUNTAINS MADE OF FUCKING FIRE. THE PALACE IS GUARDED BY A GIANT PANTHER WITH NINE HUMAN HEADS. IT'S A FUCKING INSANE PALACE, AND HUANG TI HAS NO SENSE OF STYLE. HE'S AN EMPEROR, THOUGH, SO HE CAN DO WHATEVER THE FUCK HE WANTS.

THE RED EMPEROR IS METAL AS FUCK

THE RED EMPEROR IS THE GOD OF MOTHERFUCKING FIRE AND METAL AND THE SUN. HE'S PRETTY FUCKING COOL. HE'S ALSO KIND OF EVIL AND TRIES TO OVERTHROW THE YELLOW EMPEROR A FEW TIMES, BUT NOBODY GIVES A SHIT ABOUT THAT.

WHEN HE FIRST ARRIVES ON EARTH, HE SETS UP A FUCKING MASSIVE FIRE CASTLE AND THEN GOES OUT TO SEE HOW SHIT EVERYTHING IS FOR THE PEOPLE. IT'S PRETTY FUCKING SHIT; THEY DON'T HAVE ENOUGH FOOD OR ANYTHING LIKE THAT.

HE STARTS BY TEACHING THE PEOPLE METALWORKING SO THEY CAN MURDER THE SHIT OUT OF ALL THE POISONOUS SNAKES EVERYWHERE, AND THEN GETS THEM TO PLOUGH THE GROUND AROUND HIS KINGDOM.

THEN HE DECIDES HE NEEDS MORE PLANTS, SO HE FUCKING SHOUTS AT THE BIRDS UNTIL THEY SURRENDER AND GIVE HIM A FUCK-TONNE OF SEEDS, AND THEN HE PLANTS A FIELD.

NOT HAPPY WITH HOW MUCH FOOD THERE IS, HE MAKES A MOTHERFUCKING FIRE WHIP AND WHIPS THE SHIT OUT OF THE PLANTS UNTIL THEY MAGICALLY DEVELOP HEALING POWERS. THE RED EMPEROR IS ONE BADASS MOTHERFUCKER.

ALL THE PEOPLE LOVE HIM TO BITS, AND ARE ALSO FUCKING TERRIFIED OF HIM BECAUSE HE'S A FUCKING MANIAC WITH A WHIP MADE OUT OF MOTHERFUCKING FIRE, SO THEY MAKE A GIANT CAULDRON TO SHOW JUST HOW FUCKING MUCH THEY LOVE HIM, AND HE'S HAPPY AND DOESN'T BEAT THE SHIT OUT OF HIM. AND THAT'S HOW YOU RULE A KINGDOM, BITCHES.

LIFEGUARDS? HA HA FUCK NO

THE RED EMPEROR HAS THREE DAUGHTERS, AND HE FUCKING LOVES ALL OF THEM. THE YOUNGEST IS HIS FAVOURITE THOUGH, AND HE NAMES HER NU WA, AFTER THE CRAZY FUCKING SNAKE GODDESS. NU WA IS FUCKING ADORABLE, AND EVERYONE LOVES HER.

ONE DAY, NU WA DECIDES TO GO FOR A SWIM. THE WATER IS SPARKLY AS FUCK AND LOOKS PRETTY, AND THE BIRDS ARE HONKING MERRILY. SHE DIVES INTO THE WATER AND SPLASHES ABOUT FOR A BIT. AFTER A WHILE, THOUGH, SHE REALISES THAT SHE'S FUCKED UP AND DRIFTED MILES FROM SHORE. THEN A FUCKING STORM HAPPENS AND SHE DROWNS. IT'S TRAGIC AND GENERALLY PRETTY SHITTY.

HER SPIRIT ESCAPES, THOUGH, AND POSSESSES A NEARBY BIRD. NU WA IS REALLY FUCKING ANGRY AT THE SEA FOR KILLING HER, SO SHE VOWS REVENGE. SHE'S THE ANGRIEST FUCKING BIRD IN THE WORLD. SHE'S PROBABLY A SEAGULL. SEAGULLS ARE ASSHOLES.

NU WA SETS OUT TO FILL THE MOTHERFUCKING SEA. EVERY DAY, SHE FLIES TO THE SHORE, COLLECTS A BUNCH OF STICKS AND STONES, FLIES OUT TO SEA AGAIN, AND DROPS THEM IN. IT'S NOT VERY EFFECTIVE, BUT SHE KEEPS GOING. SHE'S AN IMMORTAL ANGRY REVENGE BIRD, SO SHE'S STILL GOING NOW, FLYING BACKWARDS AND FORWARDS DROPPING SHIT IN THE SEA. SHE'S A STUBBORN FUCK.

MAGICAL FOOT PREGNANCY

THE GREEN EMPEROR'S BIRTH IS REALLY, REALLY FUCKED UP.

HIS MOTHER IS A MORTAL CALLED HUA XU, WHO'S JUST A NORMAL BORING PERSON. ONE DAY, SHE GOES FOR A WALK IN THE SWAMP; WHILE SHE'S OUT SHE FINDS A FUCKING MASSIVE FOOTPRINT. IT'S REALLY FUCKING MASSIVE AND SHE HASN'T A FUCKING CLUE WHAT COULD HAVE MADE IT. SHE GETS REALLY EXCITED ABOUT THE THOUGHT OF WHAT SORT OF CRAZY FUCKING MONSTER COULD HAVE MADE IT, AND DECIDES TO COMPARE IT TO THE SIZE OF HER FOOT. SHE STEPS INTO THE FOOTPRINT, AND SUDDENLY FEELS ALL TINGLY AND WEIRD.

WHEN SHE GETS HOME, SHE DISCOVERS THAT SUDDENLY SHE'S MAGICALLY PREGNANT. WHAT THE FUCK?

NINE MONTHS LATER SHE GIVES BIRTH TO A SNAKE WITH A HUMAN FACE. SHE LOVES HER MUTANT SNAKE BABY TO BITS, AND CALLS IT TAI HOU. WHEN TAI HOU THE MUTANT SNAKE BABY GROWS UP, HE BECOMES THE GREEN EMPEROR, DESPITE BEING A MOTHERFUCKING SNAKE THING.

XING TIAN THE HEADLESS GIANT

XING TIAN IS AN ANGRY GIANT. HE SPENDS ALL HIS SPARE TIME FUCKING SHIT UP, AND THAT'S NOT GOOD. AFTER A WHILE, HE DECIDES HE'S GOING TO GO AND FUCK UP THE YELLOW EMPEROR, SO HE GETS A FUCKING MASSIVE AXE AND SETS OUT TO BEAT THE SHIT OUT OF THE YELLOW EMPEROR.

THE YELLOW EMPEROR HEARS HIM COMING, AND GETS OUT A FUCKING MASSIVE SWORD. HE GOES OUT TO MEET XING TIAN, AND THE TWO OF THEM HAVE A FUCKING MASSIVE FIGHT UP IN THE MOUNTAINS. IT GOES ON FOR FUCKING DAYS, AND IN THE END THE YELLOW EMPEROR WINS AND HACKS THE HEAD OFF THE GIANT.

THAT'S NOT ENOUGH, THOUGH, BECAUSE XING TIAN IS ONE HELL OF A TENACIOUS MOTHERFUCKER. HE FLAILS AROUND LOOKING FOR THE HEAD, SO THE YELLOW EMPEROR QUICKLY CUTS A MOUNTAIN IN HALF, DROPS THE HEAD IN THE GAP, AND SEALS THAT SHIT UP AGAIN.

AFTER THAT, XING TIAN THE HEADLESS GIANT WANDERS THE EARTH LOOKING FOR HIS HEAD AND FUCKING SHIT UP ON THE WAY. HE'S NOT BLIND, THOUGH, EVEN WITH NO HEAD. WHY? BECAUSE HE CAN SEE OUT OF HIS MOTHERFUCKING NIPPLES, THAT'S WHY.

FLAMING FIRE BABIES

DIJUN, THE GOD OF THE EAST, IS MARRIED TO XIHE, THE SUN GODDESS, AND THEY LIVE ON THE FUCKING BEACH ALL THE WAY TO THE FAR EAST OF THE WORLD. SOON AFTER THE WEDDING, XIHE GIVES BIRTH TO TEN BEAUTIFUL BABIES.

EXCEPT THEY AREN'T BABIES. THEY'RE MOTHERFUCKING SUNS. SHE GIVES BIRTH TO TEN FUCKING MASSIVE BALLS OF FIRE. WHAT THE FUCK? DIJUN IS NO LONGER CERTAIN HE'S THE FATHER.

XIHE PUTS ALL TEN SUNS IN A TREE, SO THEY CAN FROLIC MERRILY IN THE WAY THAT ALL SUNS FUCKING LOVE TO DO, AND SO THEY CAN DIVE INTO THE SEA WHEN THEY GET TOO HOT. SHE'S A FUCKING GREAT MOTHER. EVERY DAY SHE CHOOSES ONE OF HER FIREBALL BABIES TO BE THE SUN FOR THE DAY, AND TAKES IT TO WORK WHERE IT LIGHTS UP THE WORLD.

AFTER A WHILE, THOUGH THE SUN BABIES ARE FED UP WITH THIS SHIT. THEY WANT TO FROLIC ALL TOGETHER IN A GROUP OF TEN, NOT IN A GROUP OF NINE WITH ONE HAVING TO WORK. SUNS ARE FUCKING STUPID INCONSIDERATE LITTLE SHITS, SO THEY ALL DECIDE TO REBEL AND ALL DIVE INTO THE SKY TOGETHER. THEY FROLIC HAPPILY IN THE SKY ALL DAY, BUT THAT'S A FUCKING DISASTER FOR THE WORLD BELOW.

ALL THE RIVERS DRY UP, THE PLANTS DIE, THE MONSTERS EMERGE FROM THE GROUND, HALF THE PEOPLE GET EATEN, AND EVERYTHING IS GENERALLY SHIT. THE FIRE BABIES REALLY FUCKED UP, BUT THEY DON'T GIVE A SHIT. THEY'RE INCONSIDERATE FUCKS.

MURDERING BABIES

AFTER THEIR INSANE FIRE BABIES BURN THE FUCKING EARTH DRY, DIJUN AND XIHE CALL ON HOU YI, THE ARCHER GOD, TO FIX THE SHIT THEIR KIDS FUCKED UP. THEY TELL HIM TO DO WHATEVER HE HAS TO DO TO MAKE THE WORLD LESS SHIT, BUT HE MUSTN'T KILL THE BABY SUNS. HE SHOULD SHOOT THE SHIT OUT OF ALL THE SCARY MONSTERS THOUGH.

HOU YI TAKES HIS WIFE ON HOLIDAY TO EARTH, AND FINDS ALL THE PEOPLE WANDERING AROUND ON FIRE AND STARVING. IT'S FUCKED UP DOWN THERE. THE MORE SHIT HE SEES, THE ANGRIER HOU YI GETS. IN THE END HE'S SO FUCKING FURIOUS THAT HE CAN'T TAKE BEING SENSIBLE ANY MORE, AND STARTS TO SHOOT THE SHIT OUT OF THE BABY SUNS. FUCKING WHOOPS.

HE MURDERS NINE OF THE TEN BABIES BEFORE THE EMPEROR REALISES HE'S NOT MEANT TO BE KILLING THE FUCKING SUN BABIES AND STEALS ALL HIS FUCKING ARROWS.

PLEASED WITH WHAT HE'S DONE, AND CONVENIENTLY FORGETTING THAT HE'S BEEN TOLD NOT TO KILL ANY OF THE FUCKING SUN BABIES, HOU YI RETURNS TO HEAVEN, EXPECTING A HERO'S WELCOME... UNFORTUNATELY FOR HIM, DIJUN AND XIHE ARE FUCKING FURIOUS THAT HE MURDERED THEIR BABIES AND BANISH HIM AND HIS WIFE TO EARTH, STRIPPING THEM OF THEIR FUCKING GODLINESS.

OF COURSE, WHEN CHANG E (HOU YI'S WIFE) HEARS ABOUT THIS, SHE'S ALSO FUCKING FURIOUS. HOU YI REALLY FUCKED UP THIS TIME. THE TWO OF THEM LIVE TOGETHER ON EARTH IN COMPLETE MISERY BECAUSE THEIR LIVES ARE SHIT, UNTIL EVENTUALLY CHANG E TELLS HOU YI THAT SHE'S LEAVING HIM IF HE DOESN'T FIX HIS FUCK-UP.

NOT WANTING TO LOSE HIS WIFE, EVEN THOUGH SHE'S FUCKING HORRIBLE, HOU YI SETS OUT TO GET SOME MAGIC GOD POTION FROM THE QUEEN OF THE WEST. THE QUEEN OF THE WEST IS A REALLY FUCKING UGLY HALF-HUMAN, HALF-LEOPARD, HALF-DRAGON MONSTER. FORTUNATELY FOR HOU YI, SHE'S A FUCKING DELIGHT. SHE GIVES HIM A BOTTLE OF

MAGIC POTION, AND TELLS HIM THAT IF HE SHARES IT WITH HIS WIFE THEY'LL BOTH BE FUCKING IMMORTAL, BUT IF ONLY ONE PERSON DRINKS IT THEY'LL BECOME A REAL FUCKING GOD AGAIN.

OF COURSE, AS SOON AS HOU YI GOES OUT, CHANG E DRINKS THE WHOLE FUCKING THING AND FLOATS INTO THE SKY TO BECOME A GOD. HALF WAY UP, THOUGH, SHE REALISES THAT ALL THE OTHER GODS ARE GOING TO FUCKING HATE HER, SO SHE GOES TO THE MOON INSTEAD OF TO HEAVEN BECAUSE SHE'S A FUCKING COWARD. THEN, BECAUSE NOBODY ELSE LIVES ON THE MOON APART FROM A REALLY FUCKING BORING RABBIT, SHE TURNS INTO A FROG OUT OF LONELINESS. IT'S TRAGIC AND FUCKED UP, BUT SHE DESERVES IT. AND THAT'S WHY YOU DON'T FUCK WITH THE GODS.

HORSE + GIRL = WORST LOVE STORY EVER

THERE'S A WAR ON SOMEWHERE AT THE EDGE OF CHINA, SO ALL THE MEN IN THE WHOLE FUCKING COUNTRY HAVE TO GO AND FIGHT. NO, THIS ISN'T MULAN. IT'S WAY MORE FUCKED UP AND DOESN'T HAVE AS MUCH CROSS-DRESSING.

ONE MAN LEAVES HIS FAMILY BEHIND AND TELLS HIS DAUGHTER TO LOOK AFTER HIS FAVOURITE HORSE. WHAT HE DOESN'T KNOW IS THAT HIS HORSE IS PRETTY FUCKING WEIRD AND IS IN LOVE WITH HIS DAUGHTER.

ONE DAY, WHILE SHE'S BRUSHING THE HORSE, THE GIRL SAYS SHE MISSES HER FATHER SO FUCKING MUCH THAT SHE'LL MARRY WHOEVER BRINGS HIM BACK TO HER. SEEING HIS CHANCE, THE HORSE IMMEDIATELY BREAKS HIS ROPES AND FUCKS OFF.

A FEW DAYS LATER, THE HORSE COMES HOME WITH HER FATHER, AND LOOKS REALLY FUCKING SMUG. WHEN HER FATHER FINDS OUT WHAT HAPPENED, HE'S REALLY FUCKING ANGRY AND LOCKS HER IN HER ROOM. THE HORSE THEN DIES OF SADNESS, AND HE LETS HER OUT OF HER ROOM BECAUSE IT'S FUCKING DEAD SO SHE CAN'T MARRY IT.

AS SOON AS SHE LEAVES HER ROOM, THOUGH, THE HORSE'S DEAD BODY WRAPS ITSELF AROUND HER AND DRAGS HER INTO THE NEAREST BUSH. NOT FOR WILD HORSEY SEX, THOUGH. WHEN IT REACHES THE BUSH, THE HORSE CORPSE VANISHES, LEAVING ONLY THE DAUGHTER. SHE'S TURNED INTO A MOTHERFUCKING SILKWORM. HER FATHER TAKES THE SILKWORM HOME AND CONTINUES TO LOVE IT JUST AS MUCH AS HE DID WHEN IT WAS HIS DAUGHTER, WHICH IS A BIT WEIRD BUT AT LEAST IT'S A HAPPY SILKWORM.

JAPANESE MYTHOLOGY

BEGINNINGS: AINU STYLE

IN THE BEGINNING, ALL THERE IS IS FUCKLOADS OF WATER. AS USUAL. THE GODS SEND DOWN A BIRD TO SORT THAT SHIT OUT, AND THE BIRD FLAPS ABOUT JUST ABOVE THE WATER. ITS WINGS BLOW THE WATER ASIDE, AND ISLANDS APPEAR. FUCK YES.

THERE ARE STILL NO PEOPLE, THOUGH, SO THE GODS HAVE TO POPULATE THE WORLD. DO THEY CREATE A MAN AND THE WOMAN TO POPULATE THE WORLD? FUCK NO. BEARS. THEY POPULATE THE WORLD ENTIRELY WITH MOTHERFUCKING BEARS. THEY'RE EVERYWHERE, DOING BEAR THINGS AND BEING HAIRY AND SLIGHTLY MENACING.

THE BEARS GO ON TO HAVE HAIRY HUMAN BABIES IN THE END, AND THAT'S WHY THE AINU ARE HAIRIER THAN ANYONE ELSE IN JAPAN, BUT MOST FUCKING THINGS ARE STILL BEARS. THEY'RE FUCKING EVERYWHERE. IS THAT A DOG? NO, IT'S A FUCKING BEAR. TABLE? NO. BEAR. PERSON? NO. ANOTHER FUCKING BEAR. EVERYTHING IS BEARS. BE VERY FUCKING AFRAID.

MEDICINE IS DANGEROUS

SOMEWHERE IN JAPAN, A WOMAN FALLS ILL. NOBODY HAS A FUCKING CLUE WHAT SHE'S CAUGHT, BUT IT'S ONE HELL OF A LOT DEADLIER THAN A NORMAL BORING COLD, AND IT LOOKS LIKE SHE'S GOING TO DIE.

HER HUSBAND WANDERS AROUND LOOKING FOR SOMEONE THAT MIGHT POSSIBLY KNOW A CURE FOR HER MYSTERY FATAL ILLNESS, BUT NOBODY KNOWS. EVERYTHING IS SHIT, AND HE RETURNS HOME IN DESPAIR. ON HIS WAY, THOUGH, HE RUNS INTO AN OLD MAN WHO TELLS HIM TO GIVE HER THE POWDERED LIVER OF A WHITE DOG. HE DOES SO, AND SHE'S FUCKING FINE.

A WHILE LATER, THE WOMAN GIVES BIRTH TO A HAPPY HEALTHY BABY GIRL, AND FOR A FEW YEARS EVERYTHING IS FUCKING GREAT. EVENTUALLY, SOMEONE NOTICES THAT TRAVELLERS IN THE AREA ARE GOING MISSING, AND A WATCH IS SET UP TO KEEP AN EYE OUT FOR MURDERERS. IT TURNS OUT THAT EVERY NIGHT WHEN EVERYONE IS ASLEEP, THE LITTLE GIRL'S FUCKING HEAD COMES OFF AND FLOATS AROUND THE VILLAGE LOOKING FOR BLOOD.

THAT'S WHAT HAPPENS TO THE TRAVELLERS. THEY GET FUCKING EATEN BY THE MOTHERFUCKING SEVERED FLOATING HEAD OF A LITTLE GIRL. IN THE END THE HEAD GETS EATEN BY A PASSING DOG, AND IT'S ALL FINE AGAIN. EXCEPT NOW THE COUPLE ARE LEFT WITH A HEADLESS CORPSE INSTEAD OF A DAUGHTER. IT'S BETTER THAN THE TOWN BEING TERRORISED BY A MOTHERFUCKING EVIL FLOATING BLOODSUCKING HEAD THOUGH.

ISLAND BABIES

IZANAGI AND IZANAMI ARE THE SEVENTH GENERATION OF DIVINE HUSBAND AND WIFE DUOS. AT THIS POINT EARTH IS STILL A LIQUIDY MESS BECAUSE THE PREVIOUS GODS HAD JUST FUCKED AROUND AND HIDDEN IN A CORNER.

BUT THIS COUPLE MEAN SERIOUS BUSINESS, AND TOGETHER THEY STIR THE OCEAN WITH A FUCKING BIG STICK. FROM DOING THIS, THE EARTH STARTS TO SOLIDIFY AND FORMS THE ISLAND OF ONOKORO, A PERFECT FIRST HOME FOR A NICE YOUNG COUPLE.

THEY BUILD A HOUSE THERE AND A FUCKING GREAT POLE, BECAUSE EVERYONE NEEDS A FUCKING GREAT POLE. THEY THEN REALISE THEY SHOULD PROBABLY GET ON WITH THE WHOLE POPULATING THE EARTH FUCKERY, SO THEY DO A SEXY LITTLE ~~POLE DANCE~~ WALK AROUND THE POLE, MEETING EACH OTHER IN THE MIDDLE.

IZANAMI GREETS IZANAGI, "YOU LOOK DAMN FINE" SHE SAYS, BUT IZANAGI IS SUPER PISSED AT THIS BECAUSE HE SHOULD HAVE GREETED HER FIRST AND THIS IS SERIOUS RITUAL STUFF.

NEVERTHELESS THEY FUCK ANYWAY. THEIR FIRST TWO KIDS ARE GENERALLY CRAP AND SO THEIR PARENTS JUST FUCKING ABANDON THEM, LETTING THEM CRAWL OFF AND BECOME SHITTY ISLANDS.

THE OTHER GODS TELL THEM THAT THESE UGLY-ASS CHILDREN ARE BECAUSE THEY DIDN'T DO THE POLE-DANCING RITUAL RIGHT, SO THEY REPEAT IT AND IZANAGI SPEAKS FIRST THIS TIME.

THEY THEN HAVE EIGHT PERFECT ISLAND BABIES AND A BUNCH OF OTHER GODS AND EVERYTHING'S FINE. FOR NOW.

IZANAGI HAS ZOMBIE WIFE PROBLEMS

THE LAST OF IZANAGI AND IZANAMI'S KIDS TOGETHER IS THE GOD OF FIRE. FIRE DEITIES TEND TO BE ACTUALLY ON FUCKING FIRE, SO UNFORTUNATELY THIS MEANS THAT IZANAMI IS FUCKING BURNT TO DEATH AS THE BABY IS BORN.

IZANAGI FUCKING LOVED HIS WIFE AND IS HELLA MAD AT THIS. HIS MANLY TEARS EVEN BECOME ANOTHER GODDESS. HE QUICKLY DECIDES THAT THE CAUSE OF ALL THIS SHIT IS THE FIRE-BABY, SO HE CUTS ITS FUCKING HEAD OFF. OUCH.

BITS OF THE BABY'S BLOOD AND BODY ALL FORM YET MORE GODS AND NOW THERE'S A GOD FOR JUST ABOUT EVERYTHING YOU COULD EVER FUCKING WANT.

OF COURSE, THIS DOESN'T SATISFY IZANAGI. HE JUST WANTS HIS WIFE BACK, SO HE GOES TO YOMI, THE LAND OF THE DEAD, TO RESCUE HER. WHAT A FUCKING SWEETHEART.

BY THE TIME HE FINDS HER, SHE'S ALREADY EATEN THE FOOD DOWNSTAIRS (SOUND FAMILIAR?) AND SO TOUGH SHIT, SHE CAN'T COME HOME. SHE ALSO TELLS IZANAGI NOT TO LOOK AT HER, BUT HE DOES ANYWAY AND SHE'S ALL GROSS AND HELLA DEAD. WHAT A FUCKING SURPRISE.

THIS PISSES IZANAMI OFF BECAUSE SHE'S ASHAMED OF HOW DEAD SHE IS, SO SHE SETS A BUNCH OF NASTY SPIRITS ON IZANAGI. HE THROWS PEACHES AT THEM AND FUCKS OFF.

SHE FOLLOWS HIM TO THE ENTRANCE OF YOMI, WHICH IS A SERIOUS FUCKING PROBLEM BECAUSE YOU CAN'T JUST HAVE ZOMBIE GODDESSES FUCKING AROUND IN THE WORLD OF THE LIVING. IZANAGI PUTS IN A BIGASS ROCK TO STOP HER ESCAPING. SHE PROMISES TO KILL LOTS OF FUCKERS, HE PROMISES TO CREATE LOTS OF FUCKERS AND THEY GET A DIVORCE.

IZANAGI FINALLY GETS HOME AND HAS A WELL-DESERVED WASH IN A RIVER. OF COURSE ANYTIME IZANAGI DOES ANYTHING HE ENDS UP CREATING A SHIT-TONNE MORE GODS,

SO NEW ONES POP UP FROM HIS PILE OF CLOTHES, EYES AND MOUTH AND BASICALLY EVERYWHERE.

TAIRA NO MASAKADO MURDERS EVERYONE

TAIRA NO MASAKADO IS A SAMURAI FROM A RICH FAMILY, AND HE'S A MOTHERFUCKING BADASS MANIAC SERIAL KILLER.

ONE DAY, HIS UNCLE TRIES TO DISPOSE OF HIM, SO TAIRA NO MASAKADO MURDERS HIM TO DEATH, KILLS ALL HIS FAMILY, BURNS ALL HIS FIELDS AND DESTROYS ALL HIS HOUSES. IT'S A BIT OF AN OVERREACTION, SO HE GETS BROUGHT TO TRIAL. SURPRISE, BITCHES! ALL THAT MURDER WAS LEGAL, AND TAIRA NO MASAKADO IS LET OFF AND ALLOWED TO GO HOME.

THEN HE MURDERS HIS FATHER-IN-LAW. AND HIS COUSINS. AND THEN HE TAKES OVER EIGHT FUCKING PROVINCES. IT'S STILL ALL LEGAL, THOUGH, SO NOBODY CAN DO A FUCKING THING TO STOP HIM FROM MURDERING EVERYONE.

THEN HE DECLARES HIMSELF EMPEROR. WHOOPS. FUNNILY ENOUGH, THAT'S NOT FUCKING LEGAL. THE GOVERNMENT HAVE HIM ASSASSINATED AND HE GETS BEHEADED. IS THAT GOING TO STOP HIS REIGN OF TERROR AND MURDER? FUCK NO.

SEVERAL MONTHS LATER, HIS SEVERED HEAD STARTS SHOUTING ABOUT WANTING ITS BODY BACK. THEN IT LIGHTS UP AND FLIES OFF, UNTIL IT EVENTUALLY GETS REALLY FUCKING TIRED AND LANDS. UNTIL THE HEAD GETS PROPERLY BURIED, THOUGH, IT CONTINUES TO FUCK SHIT UP. IT CAUSES A PLAGUE, AN EARTHQUAKE, AND SEVERAL FREAK DEATHS. EVENTUALLY, IN A DESPERATE ATTEMPT TO MAKE HIM CALM THE FUCK DOWN AND STOP MURDERING PEOPLE, TAIRA NO MASAKADO'S SEVERED GHOST HEAD IS DECLARED A GHOST. IN 1984. THAT'S ONE HELL OF A LOT OF ANGRY MURDER GHOST CARNAGE. IN THE THIRTY YEARS SINCE THEN, SHIT SEEMS TO HAVE CALMED DOWN A BIT.

KILLER FROG PRINCESS

AFTER TAIRA NO MASAKADO IS EXECUTED FOR MURDERING EVERYONE AND DECLARING HIMSELF EMPEROR, HIS KIDS RUN AWAY AND GO INTO HIDING. HIS DAUGHTER, SATSUKI, BECOMES A REALLY SHITTY NUN. HIS SON YOSHIKADO, HOWEVER, HAS OTHER PLANS, GIVEN THAT DUDES CAN'T USUALLY BE NUNS. HE TRACKS DOWN A CRAZY-ASS OLD WIZARD WHO GIVES HIM A SCROLL CONTAINING THE SECRETS OF FROG MAGIC. THAT'S RIGHT, MOTHERFUCKING FROG MAGIC.

HE GIVES THE SCROLL TO HIS SISTER, WHO IMMEDIATELY ABANDONS BEING A NUN IN FAVOUR OF BEING A CRAZY MURDEROUS DEMON PRINCESS AND CONTINUING HER FATHER'S FUCKED-UP REIGN OF MURDERY TERROR.

IN THE END A WARRIOR CALLED MITSUKUNI SETS OUT TO STOP THE CRAZY FROG WITCH PRINCESS, BUT IT DOESN'T GO AS WELL AS HE HOPES. SHE ATTACKS HIS CASTLE WITH A FUCKING MASSIVE ARMY OF SKELETONS, INCLUDING A MAGIC GIANT SKELETON MONSTER. SHE LEADS HER FUCKING TERRIFYING SKELETON ARMY INTO BATTLE, RIDING ON THE BACK OF A FUCKING MASSIVE TOAD. UNSURPRISINGLY, MITSUKUNI GETS MURDERED TO DEATH BY A MOB OF ANGRY SKELETONS.

EVENTUALLY, THOUGH, SHE DIES AND HER REBELLION IS SQUASHED. IT'S A BIT OF A SHIT ENDING, BUT AT LEAST SHE MANAGED TO GO INTO BATTLE ON A GIANT TOAD AND LEAD A SKELETON ARMY. THAT'S A PRETTY FUCKING GREAT WAY TO GO.

DEMONIC BUTT FONDLING

JINGOBEI IS A SAMURAI. HE LIVES IN A FANCY-ASS HOUSE WITH A WORKING TOILET. IT'S PRETTY FUCKING GREAT. ONE DAY, WHEN HIS WIFE GOES TO THE TOILET, SHE FEELS SOMETHING REACH UP OUT OF THE TOILET AND STROKE HER BUTT AFFECTIONATELY.

SHE'S PRETTY FUCKING FREAKED OUT AND TELLS JINGOBEI, WHO DECIDES THAT IT MUST BE A DEMON AND WAITS BY THE TOILET TO AMBUSH THE BUTT-STROKING DEMON. SOON A FUCKING MASSIVE HAIRY ARM REACHES OUT OF THE TOILET AND WAGGLES AROUND, LOOKING FOR A BUTT TO STROKE. JINGOBEI CUTS IT OFF AND GOES TO FIND AN EXPERT TO TELL HIM WHY A DEMON WANTS TO STROKE HIS WIFE'S BUTT.

THE FIRST PRIEST HE SHOWS THE ARM TO HASN'T A FUCKING CLUE WHAT'S GOING ON. THE SECOND ONE IDENTIFIES IT AS THE ARM OF A KUROTE, A HAIRY DEMON THAT LIVES IN TOILETS AND LIKES TO STROKE BUTTS. THE THIRD PRIEST STARES AT THE ARM, TRANSFORMS INTO A FUCKING MASSIVE HAIRY MONSTER, GRABS THE ARM, STICKS IT ONTO THE SHOULDER STUMP THAT JINGOBEI FAILED TO NOTICE, AND FUCKS OFF INTO THE NIGHT TO FIND A SAFER BUTT TO STROKE.

DICKS ON PARADE

KANAMARA MATSURI (FESTIVAL OF THE STEEL DICK) IS A YEARLY FESTIVAL IN KAWASAKI, JAPAN. LONG STORY SHORT, THERE'S A FUCKING MASSIVE WOODEN DICK THAT GETS PARADED THROUGH THE STREETS TO A SHRINE AND THERE'S A BIGASS PARTY. SOUNDS FUCKING GREAT.

THE MYTH BEHIND IT IS ALSO FUCKTASTIC. SOME NICE YOUNG GIRL GETS HER FUCKING VAGINA POSSESSED BY A BITEY DEMON WITH SHARP TEETH. ALTERNATIVELY, THE GIRL IS A BITEY-VAGINA DEMON HERSELF (WATCH OUT FOR THOSE).

SHE GETS MARRIED NOT ONCE BUT TWICE AND BOTH TIMES HER VAG GETS BITEY ON THEIR WEDDING NIGHT AND IT BITES EVERYONE'S DICK OFF. UNDERSTANDABLY ALL THE MENFOLK RUN THE FUCK AWAY FROM THIS SHIT. THIS KINDA SUCKED FOR HER BECAUSE SHE WAS TOTALLY IN LOVE WITH SOME DUDE.

SO SHE GOES TO A BLACKSMITH AND ASKS HIM TO MAKE HER A BIG METAL DILDO TO FUCKING DESTROY THOSE TEETH. CLEARLY THIS SHIT WAS WAY TOO NASTY FOR A DENTIST. HE MAKES THIS FOR HER, NO QUESTIONS ASKED, AND SHE USES IT TO DESTROY HER FANG DEMON PROBLEM, MARRIES THE MAN SHE LOVES AND LIVES HAPPILY EVER AFTER.

THE METAL DICK IS THEN PUT IN A SHRINE AND FOLKS START WORSHIPPING IT AS A FERTILITY/ ANTI-SYPHILIS SYMBOL. FUCK YES METAL DICKS SAVE THE DAY.

PIRATES VS SNAILS

A CREW OF PIRATES ARE FUCKING AROUND AND DOING PIRATE THINGS WHEN THEY SEE A BEAUTIFUL GIRL FLOATING IN THE SEA BY THEIR BOAT. THEY PULL HER OUT OF THE WATER BECAUSE THEY'RE A BUNCH OF HORNY FUCKS AND SHE'S REALLY FUCKING HOT, BUT THEY DON'T STOP TO CONSIDER WHY THE FUCK SHE WAS IN THERE IN THE FIRST PLACE.

ONE BY ONE THEY TAKE HER BACK TO THEIR CABINS FOR SEXY SEX, AND ONE BY ONE THEY REALISE JUST HOW MUCH THEY'VE FUCKED UP. SHE'S NOT A REAL GIRL, SHE'S A SAZAE-ONI. SHE'S A MOTHERFUCKING MAN-EATING DEMON SNAIL IN DISGUISE. SHE WORKS HER WAY THROUGH THE CREW, BITING OFF THEIR MOTHERFUCKING TESTICLES AND MAKING ANGRY SNAIL NOISES.

EVENTUALLY, THE PIRATES ARE ALL SO FUCKING UPSET THAT THEY'VE LOST THEIR BALLS THAT THEY PAY HER ALL OF THEIR TREASURE TO GET THEIR BALLS BACK. THE SAZAE-ONI STICKS THE GOLD IN HER SHELL AND SLITHERS OFF BACK INTO THE SEA, LEAVING THE PIRATES HOLDING THEIR BALLS AND LOOKING SAD AND CONFUSED.

AND THAT'S WHY YOU SHOULDN'T TRY TO FUCK A SNAIL.

FINNISH MYTHOLOGY

BEGINNINGS: FINNISH STYLE

IN THE BEGINNING, ALL THERE IS IS THE SEA. FUCKLOADS OF WATER, STRETCHING OUT FOR MILES AND MILES. THERE AREN'T EVEN ANY FISH. IT'S SHIT.

ILMATAR, THE AIR SPIRIT, DECIDES TO HAVE A BATH IN THE SEA. SHE SITS DOWN IN IT, AND IMMEDIATELY GETS PREGNANT. IT'S A BIT FUCKING WEIRD, BUT HEY, IT'S NOT GOING TO MAKE HER GET OUT OF THE BATH.

AFTER A WHILE A PASSING DUCK SEES ILMATAR'S KNEE STICKING OUT OF THE SEA AND LAYS EGGS ON IT, BECAUSE DUCKS ARE FUCKING STUPID AND CAN'T TELL WHERE A SENSIBLE PLACE TO NEST MIGHT BE. THE EGGS GET HOTTER AND HOTTER FOR NO APPARENT REASON, AND ILMATAR STARTS TO WORRY THAT HER KNEE MIGHT BE ON FIRE. SHE SHAKES HER LEG, AND THE EGGS FLY OFF HER KNEE. DO THEY BREAK? FUCK NO. THIS IS FINLAND, WHERE EVEN THE DUCKS ARE METAL AS FUCK. THE EGGS SHATTER IN A MOTHERFUCKING EXPLOSION, AND THE SHARDS OF MAGIC DUCK EGG TURN INTO THE LAND AND SKY AND CLOUDS AND SHIT LIKE THAT. FINNISH DUCKS ARE FUCKING SCARY.

HOW DOES FARMING WORK? FIRE. THAT'S HOW.

VAINAMOINEN, WHO IS BASICALLY GANDALF, IS BORED AS FUCK. HIS MOTHER ILMATAR HAS BEEN PREGNANT WITH HIM FOR AGES, AND HE WANTS TO GET OUT AND LET HIS BEARD FLY FREE IN THE WIND. HE'S HAD ENOUGH OF THIS WOMB BULLSHIT, SO HE BEATS THE SHIT OUT OF HIS MOTHER FROM INSIDE UNTIL HE FALLS OUT, AND THEN HE POSES DRAMATICALLY ON THE BEACH WITH HIS BEARD FLAPPING HEROICALLY IN THE WIND FOR A BIT.

VAINAMOINEN LOOKS AT THE WORLD AND DECIDES THAT IT'S BORING AS FUCK. SURE, IT'S GOT STARS AND SHIT LIKE THAT, BUT OTHER THAN THAT THE WOMB WAS BETTER. AT LEAST IT WAS WARM IN THERE. HE SUMMONS SAMPSA PELLERVOINEN, THE GOD OF FERTILITY, AND TELLS HIM TO PLANT SOME TREES. NOW THERE ARE TREES EVERYWHERE, BUT THE OAK TREES JUST WON'T FUCKING GROW.

VAINAMOINEN SHOUTS A BIT, AND THEN SUMMONS IKU-TURSO, WHO'S A MOTHERFUCKING GIANT WALRUS MONSTER. IKU-TURSO SETS FIRE TO SOME SHIT AND PLANTS AN ACORN IN THE ASHES. IT GROWS INTO AN OAK TREE, BUT IT DOESN'T FUCKING STOP. IT GROWS UP TO HEAVEN AND BLOCKS OUT ALL THE FUCKING SUNLIGHT. VAINAMOINEN ISN'T HAPPY AT ALL, BUT IT'S HIS OWN FAULT FOR THINKING THAT A MOTHERFUCKING GIANT WALRUS MONSTER KNOWS ANYTHING ABOUT TREES.

VAINAMOINEN ASKS HIS MOTHER FOR HELP, AND SHE SENDS A TINY METAL MAN TO HELP. VAINAMOINEN'S A DICK, SO HE LAUGHS AT THE METAL MAN FOR BEING SO FUCKING TINY. AT THIS POINT THE METAL MAN GROWS UNTIL HIS HEAD DISAPPEARS INTO THE CLOUDS. THEN HE CUTS THE FUCKING MASSIVE OAK TREE DOWN IN THREE SWINGS, AND FUCKS OFF BACK INTO THE SEA.

THEN VAINAMOINEN REALISES THAT HIS CROPS WON'T GROW, SO HE CUTS DOWN ALL THE TREES EXCEPT ONE, WHICH HE LEAVES FOR THE BIRDS TO NEST IN. HE HAS A FUNDAMENTAL

MISUNDERSTANDING OF HOW MANY FUCKING BIRDS CAN FIT ONTO ONE TREE, BUT THEY'RE SO GRATEFUL THAT HE THOUGHT OF THEM THAT THEY BURN THE SHIT OUT OF ALL THE MOTHERFUCKING FALLEN TREES, AND VAINAMOINEN'S CROPS START GROWING IN THE ASHES.

RAP BATTLE WITH GANDALF

A KID CALLED JOUKAHAINEN THINKS HE CAN SING BETTER THAN VAINAMOINEN CAN, SO HE CHALLENGES HIM TO A SONG CONTEST. VAINAMOINEN HAS NO TIME FOR THIS SHIT; HE'S GOT IMPORTANT WIZARDLY BULLSHIT TO DO. MOST OF IT CONSISTS OF LOOKING ONE HELL OF A LOT LIKE GANDALF AND LETTING HIS BEARD FLAP DRAMATICALLY IN THE WIND, BUT HEY. IT'S STILL IMPORTANT WIZARDLY BULLSHIT.

INSTEAD OF A SONG CONTEST, VAINAMOINEN SUGGESTS A SLEDGE JOUST BECAUSE IT'S FASTER. ALSO HE REALLY FUCKING LOVES SMASHING SHIT UP WITH HIS SLEDGE.

THE TWO OF THEM SLEDGE TOWARDS EACH OTHER REALLY FUCKING FAST UNTIL THEY SMASH INTO EACH OTHER AND EVERYTHING EXPLODES. THERE ARE BITS OF SLEDGE EVERYWHERE AND A FUCKING MASSIVE HOLE IN THE GROUND. NOBODY IS DEAD, THOUGH, SO THEY HAVE A KNOWLEDGE-OFF INSTEAD.

JOUKAHAINEN LIES ABOUT ALL THE SHIT HE'S DONE, AND VAINAMOINEN STARTS TO GET PRETTY FUCKING PISSED OFF AT HIM. NEXT, THEY MOVE ON TO A SWORDFIGHT. JOUKAHAINEN CALLS VAINAMOINEN A SMELLY OLD MAN AND MAKES RUDE REMARKS ABOUT HIS MOTHER, AND AT THIS POINT VAINAMOINEN HAS HAD ENOUGH OF THIS SHIT.

HE STARTS TO SING A MAGIC WIZARD SONG, AND JOUKAHAINEN SINKS INTO THE FLOOR UP TO HIS NECK. JOUKAHAINEN FREAKS THE FUCK OUT AT THIS, BECAUSE HE'S STUCK IN THE MUD AND A SCARY OLD MAN IS SINGING MAGIC BULLSHIT SONGS AT HIM. HE BREAKS DOWN IN TEARS AND OFFER VAINAMOINEN ALL HIS GOLD, BUT VAINAMOINEN DOESN'T GIVE A FUCK. THEN HE OFFERS HIS SISTER AINO AS A WIFE, AND VAINAMOINEN ACCEPTS AND SINGS THE SONG BACKWARDS TO LET HIM OUT OF THE HOLE. VAINAMOINEN IS A CREEPY FUCK AND ALL HE REALLY WANTS OUT OF LIFE IS SEX . HE MAY LOOK LIKE GANDALF, BUT HE'S CREEPY AS FUCK.

A WIZARD'S KISS

WHEN AINO FINDS OUT THAT HER BROTHER JOUKAHAINEN HAS SOLD HER TO VAINAMOINEN THE CREEPY OLD WIZARD, SHE BREAKS DOWN IN TEARS, AND SO DOES HER MOTHER. EVERYTHING IS FUCKING TERRIBLE AND THERE'S NO WAY OUT.

SHE GOES INTO THE FOREST TO GATHER WOOD AND RUNS INTO VAINAMOINEN. HE KISSES HER, AND HIS BIG GREY BEARD IS REALLY FUCKING TICKLY AND SCRATCHY. SHE'S NOT INTO BEING FORCIBLY KISSED BY CREEPY-ASS OLD WIZARDS, SO SHE SLAPS HIM, TEARS OFF ALL HER JEWELLERY AND FUCKS OFF HOME, LEAVING HIM IN THE WOODS ALONE LOOKING A BIT CONFUSED.

THEN SHE THROWS HERSELF INTO THE SEA AND DROWNS. AND THAT'S WHY YOU SHOULDN'T KISS PEOPLE THAT AREN'T INTERESTED, EVEN IF YOU'RE BASICALLY MOTHERFUCKING GANDALF.

WIZARD HUNTING

JOUKAHAINEN VOWS REVENGE ON VAINAMOINEN FOR HITTING ON HIS SISTER SO AGGRESSIVELY THAT SHE FUCKING KILLED HERSELF. HE SPENDS YEARS MAKING A CROSSBOW OUT OF THE HORNS AND HAIR OF A MAGIC ELK, AND WAITS FOR VAINAMOINEN TO COME PAST HIS HOUSE.

HIS MOTHER TELLS HIM TO STOP BEING SUCH A FUCKING IDIOT, BECAUSE IF VAINAMOINEN DIES THEN THE SUN WILL GO OUT AND NOBODY WILL EVER BE ABLE TO SING AGAIN. VAINAMOINEN'S PRETTY FUCKING POWERFUL, BUT JOUKAHAINEN DOESN'T GIVE A FUCK AND LIES IN WAIT ANYWAY.

WHEN VAINAMOINEN COMES PAST ON HIS HORSE, JOUKAHAINEN SHOOTS AT HIM. FORTUNATELY FOR THE WORLD, HE'S A REALLY FUCKING TERRIBLE SHOT, AND THE BOLT ONLY KILLS VAINAMOINEN'S HORSE, KNOCKING HIM INTO THE RIVER.

HE FLOATS DOWNSTREAM FOR DAYS UNTIL AN EAGLE RESCUES HIM AND GIVES HIM A SLEDGE TO GET HOME WITH. HE'S HAD ENOUGH OF THIS SHIT, BUT JOUKAHAINEN IS STILL OUT THERE AND STILL WANTS TO BEAT THE SHIT OUT OF HIM.

SANTA FUCKING LOVES PORRIDGE

IN FINLAND AND SWEDEN, SANTA SHARES HIS ROLE OF CREEPY-DUDE-THAT-SNEAKS-INTO-YOUR-HOUSE-AND-GIVES-YOU-PRESENTS WITH A TINY LITTLE ONE-EYED BEARDY GNOME CREATURE THAT GLOWS IN THE DARK. HIS NAME IS TOMTE (OR TONTTU, OR NISSE), AND HE'S POSSIBLY CREEPIER THAN MOTHERFUCKING SANTA.

IN ORDER TO GET PRESENTS FROM TINY GNOME SANTA, YOU HAVE TO LEAVE HIM A FUCKING MASSIVE BOWL OF PORRIDGE WITH BUTTER ON IT IN THE HOPES THAT IT'LL KEEP HIM HAPPY. IF YOU DO IT RIGHT, HE'LL LEAVE YOU PILES OF GIFTS, BUT IF YOU FUCK IT UP THEN THE CONSEQUENCES ARE FUCKING PAINFUL.

IF YOU LEAVE HIM PORRIDGE WITH NO BUTTER, HE'LL SNEAK INTO YOUR BARN AND EAT YOUR MOTHERFUCKING COWS INSTEAD.

IF YOU EAT THE PORRIDGE YOURSELF, HE'LL SHOW UP IN A RAGE, SNEAK INTO YOUR BEDROOM, BEAT THE SHIT OUT OF YOU AND LEAVE YOU BLEEDING ON THE FLOOR. ALSO HE HAS A POISONOUS BITE.

HAVE FUN, KIDS, AND DON'T FORGET TO LEAVE PORRIDGE OUT FOR TOMTE OR FACE THE BLOODY, BRUTAL CONSEQUENCES OF FUCKING THINGS UP.

BONUS: AN INTERVIEW WITH DR. NEMESIS R. M. LIGHTSLAYER

FROM A TAPE RECORDER LEFT ANONYMOUSLY AT THE PUBLISHERS' OFFICE

I meet Dr. Lightslayer in the location we previously agreed on in our correspondence. It is not exactly what I expected; the remains of the building appear to be on fire. This may well be the café mentioned, but I struggle to make out any distinguishing features under the soot stains and claw marks. Nevertheless, Dr. Lightslayer has arrived early, and seems to be enthusiastically awaiting our interview. I attempt to order a coffee, but Dr Lightslayer appears to have already consumed the barista. Abandoning all hope of getting a drink, I turn to my guest and begin our interview.

When you were a hatchling, did you expect to grow up to run a popular mythology blog?

WHEN WE WERE A MOTHERFUCKING HATCHLING WE EXPECTED NOTHING MORE THAN BURNING AND CARNAGE. OF COURSE, WE DO ALL THAT SHIT AS WELL AS RUNNING THE BLOG. WE'RE A PRETTY FUCKING MODERN AND PROGRESSIVE DRAGON.

What do you hoard?

MOTHERFUCKING BITCOINS. AND ALSO SOMETIMES AMAZON CREDIT.

Do you breathe fire?

FUCK OFF. *[Dr. Lightslayer looks around and gestures at the smouldering rubble surrounding us]*

What is your opinion on the state of the Greek economy?

THIS SORT OF SHIT IS JUST WHAT HAPPENS WHEN YOU UNIFY YOUR FUCKING CITY STATES.

Who would win in a fight: You or Smaug?

SMAUG IS A FUCKING FICTIONAL CHARACTER. ARE YOU GOING TO KEEP WASTING MY TIME WITH THIS SHIT OR CAN WE GET TO SOME WORTHWHILE FUCKING QUESTIONS NOW?

What are your favourite kinds of music?

WE WERE INTRODUCED TO "SCREAMO". WE DISLIKED IT. IT WAS MISLEADING. NOTHING CAN TOP THE HORRIFIED FUCKING CRIES OF THE INNOCENT.

Who is your celebrity crush?

WE INTEND TO CRUSH ALL OF THE FUCKING CELEBRITIES.

What's your favourite animal to have sacrificed to you? How do you like it prepared and which side dishes should it come with?

WELL, GOATS ARE THE CLASSIC OPTION, BUT PEOPLE ARE MORE FUCKING SATISFYING. WE'LL HAPPILY EAT ANYTHING AS LONG AS IT'S PREPARED WITH SUFFICIENT FEAR AND ALSO POTATOES.

How do you stay in shape?

MOSTLY ENTHUSIASM.

Who are you wearing this afternoon?

SHIT, YOU NOTICED THAT? THAT FUCKER'S BEEN STUCK ON OUR SPIKES SINCE WE SAT ON HIM. WE HAVEN'T A FUCKING CLUE WHO HE IS, BUT HE SEEMS TO BE PRETTY FUCKING STUCK.

Where did you grow up?

IN A FUCKING CAVE. IT WAS DARK. IT COULD HAVE BEEN ANYWHERE.

If you had to choose one god or mythical character to replace one member of the cast of the hit 2001 movie "Legally Blonde", who would it be and which character would they replace?

WE WOULD REPLACE BRUISER THE TINY DOG THING WITH HERACLES. BECAUSE IT WOULD BE FUCKING HILARIOUS.

Why did you start running your blog?

TO EXPAND OUR POTENTIAL BASE OF TRIBUTE-BEARING MINIONS.

What's your favourite beer?

THE BROWN ONE WITH ALL THE FUCKING BUBBLES.

What's your favourite mythical beer?

THE EGYPTIAN ONE THAT LOOKS LIKE MOTHERFUCKING BLOOD.

Do you have any little dragonettes running around yet?

FUCK OFF. THAT IS A VERY FUCKING OFFENSIVELY PERSONAL QUESTION. HOW WOULD YOU LIKE IT IF WE ASKED YOU IF YOU HAD ANY APE GRUBS CRAWLING AROUND YET?

What is your favourite type of dragon?

DO YOU REALISE HOW FUCKING RACIST THAT IS?

Do you get lonely on dark nights, knowing that you are the last of your kind, or was it you who betrayed the Great Ones and doomed your race?

WHAT THE FUCK HAVE YOU BEEN READING? IT'S FUCKERS WHO READ TOO MANY SHITTY FANTASY NOVELS LIKE YOU WHO GIVE DRAGONS SUCH SHITTY REPUTATIONS. YOU SHOULD BE FUCKING ASHAMED OF YOURSELF, YOU EMBARRASSING COCKTRUMPET.

What colour are your scales?

YOU'RE LOOKING RIGHT AT THEM. HOW FUCKING STUPID ARE YOU?

Why are you a dragon?

[*sounds of frustrated roaring. Screams. The crunch of bones, uncomfortably close to the microphone. The recording ends abruptly*]

MORE MYTHS CAN BE FOUND AT
WWW.OEDIPUSMOTHERFUCKINGTYRANNUS.TUMBLR.COM

THE RT. HON. DR. NEMESIS R. M. LIGHTSLAYER THE MAGNIFICENT, BREAKER OF SPINES AND TWEAKER OF UNMENTIONABLES, WAS BITTEN BY A RADIOACTIVE SPIDER AT A YOUNG AGE. THIS WAS MILDLY ANNOYING BUT DID NOT CHANGE DR. LIGHTSLAYER'S LIFE IN ANY MEANINGFUL WAY.

AS AN ORPHANED STREET DRAGON, DR. LIGHTSLAYER BEGAN THEIR CAREER IN ACADEMIA BY CONSUMING UNIVERSITY PROFESSORS. THIS LED TO A LIFELONG INTEREST IN MYTHOLOGY. THE LIFELONG INTEREST IN EXPLETIVES CAME SEPARATELY.

IN RECENT YEARS, DR. LIGHTSLAYER HAS BECOME SOMETHING OF A RECLUSE, BUT SINCE HAVING DISCOVERED THE INTERNET THEY HAVE TAKEN IT UPON THEMSELVES TO SCREAM MYTHOLOGY AT ANYONE WHO STUMBLES UPON THEIR POPULAR BLOG.

DR. LIGHTSLAYER WOULD PREFER THEIR LOCATION TO REMAIN A SECRET, IN AN ATTEMPT AT AVOIDING FANMAIL AND UNWANTED PROPOSITIONS.

THIS IS DR. LIGHTSLAYER'S SECOND BOOK.

CPSIA information can be obtained
at www.ICGtesting.com
Printed in the USA
LVOW13s2252110517
534224LV00006B/329/P